MRS. BEETON'S
COLD SWEETS

JELLIES, CREAMS, FRUIT DISHES, COLD PUDDINGS, AND ICES

(350 RECIPES)

ISBN 978-1-4067-9345-1

CONTENTS

ILLUSTRATIONS

CHAPTER I

COLD SWEETS

PREPARATION OF THE INGREDIENTS

To avoid unnecessary repetition in the actual recipes, the application of the principles of baking, boiling, steaming, etc., will be here briefly described. Individual recipes, however, to which general remarks do not apply, will be described in detail. Success in preparing dishes of this class depends more on suitable proportions, manipulation, and proper application of heat than on the materials themselves, which are usually of a simple character.

Each recipe in this book gives, as nearly as possible, the exact amount of the ingredients which comprise the dish. Such terms as " well-buttered mould," " creaming," " stiffly-whipped or whisked " will be fully explained, for the convenience of the uninitiated.

EGGS

The freshness of eggs may be tested in several ways. One ingenious apparatus is a speculum, furnished with an interior looking-glass, which renders the egg sufficiently transparent to show if it is fresh, infected, or really bad. If fresh, a clear disc is thrown ; if stale, a cloudy disc with spots ; and, if bad, a dark unsightly disc is visible. Another method of ascertaining their freshness is to hold them before a lighted candle or to strong artificial light. If the egg looks clear, it will be perfectly good ; but if there is a black spot attached to the shell it is worthless. Dried eggs (reconstituted) must be utilised when fresh eggs are unavailable or when drastic economy is essential, but they cannot be expected to give quite the same results as eggs from the nest. To an experienced buyer the size, weight and appearance of eggs indicate their value, stale eggs being considerably lighter than those newly laid. Eggs that one feels at all doubtful about should always be broken in a separate vessel from others, or *all* may be tainted.

TO WHISK WHITES OF EGGS

In separating the whites from the yolks, great care must be taken not to let the least portion of the yolks get into the whites, otherwise it will be impossible to whisk the whites firm. Put the whites in a clean, dry and cool egg-bowl or shallow basin, and keep cool until wanted. Add a pinch of salt, and whisk with an ordinary wire whisk which must be clean and perfectly dry. Increase the pace until the whites form a substantial, mossy froth.

TO WHIP CREAM

Put the cream into a cold basin, and stand in a cool place whilst whipping it. Use an ordinary wire whisk for the purpose, whip gently until the cream begins to thicken, then a little more quickly. In warm weather cream quickly turns to butter if overwhipped : should this occur, continue the whipping to make the conversion complete, and use the butter for cookery purposes. When the whipped cream is not intended for immediate use, let it drain on a hair sieve in a cool place until required.

CREAMING BUTTER AND SUGAR, OR YOLK OF EGGS AND SUGAR

Butter and sugar are pressed by means of a wooden spoon against the sides of a basin until the friction has softened the butter, and the ingredients are then stirred vigorously, keeping the bowl of the spoon constantly pressed against the sides or bottom of the basin, not alternately raised and lowered as in beating. In cold weather the butter may first be slightly warmed, but it must not be allowed to melt.

Yolks of eggs and sugar are simply stirred together until thick and creamy.

PREPARATION OF DRIED FRUIT

With the introduction of machinery for fruit-cleaning purposes, currants can be procured comparatively clean, and need only a rub in a dry cloth, and picking over to remove any larger sprigs and stones that may have escaped the machine, to render them fit for use. In almost every case washing is not at all necessary ; in fact, washing the currants deprives them of some of their goodness, and, therefore, is not only a waste of time, but waste of material. As currants do not keep for any length of time, they should never be bought in large quantities. Some cooks cling to the old method of pouring boiling water over them to plump them, afterwards draining and drying them thoroughly. Sultanas, although they are no doubt cleaned, require carefully picking over, and a good rub on a coarse sieve will remove almost the whole of the sprigs, which are a very objectionable ingredient in a pudding. Raisins should in all cases be stoned, and if a large quantity has to be prepared, a small machine suitable for the purpose can be procured from the household stores or iron-monger's. It is very effective in its operations, and frees the raisins from stones in an incredibly short time, and, contrary to the general opinion, does not take out more of the flesh of the raisins than hand-picking.

MAKING PASTRY FOR TARTS, ETC.

In Chapter VI, entitled PASTRY, will be found the fullest possible instructions for making the various necessary pastes, crusts, etc.

BAKING

In baking sweets only a moderately hot oven should be used. Exceptions to this rule are sweets with pastry, which require a hot oven, at first, to set and brown the crust ; once this is done the heat may be reduced. Sweets containing beaten white of egg, require a hot oven to make them rise. *Preparations containing eggs must never be allowed to boil.* Bake custards in a tin standing in a little water and in an oven only moderately warm. A sweet to be baked must always be made more moist than one to be steamed or boiled, for baking dries it up more than does either of the latter processes.

BOILING

To ensure perfect cooking, the following rules, which apply equally to simple, plain or rich sweets, must be observed.

1. The mould or basin must be perfectly dry and well coated with butter or fat.

2. The mixture must completely fill the mould or basin.

3. A scalded and floured cloth should be tied securely over the top of the basin, but rather loosely round any pudding not boiled in a basin.

4. The water must be boiling rapidly when the pudding is put in.

5. The water must completely cover the pudding, and be deep enough to float those boiled in cloths, otherwise a plate or saucer must be placed at the bottom of the pan.

6. As the water boils away, boiling water must be added.

7. The pudding must stand a few minutes before being turned out, in order that some of the steam may escape, and thus cause the pudding to shrink and be less liable to break.

STEAMING

Sweets steamed over water are lighter than when immersed in it, but they cook more slowly. A quicker method, and one that gives practically the same results, is to stand the pudding in a saucepan containing boiling water to about half the depth of the mould or basin, the surrounding water being frequently replenished with more boiling water. A pudding to be steamed should not more than three-quarters fill the basin; and two folds of paper, made waterproof by being rubbed with butter or fat, should cover the top instead of a cloth which prevents the pudding rising.

PREPARATION OF MOULDS

Moulds, whether intended for creams or jellies, should be thoroughly clean, and when possible rinsed with cold water, before being used. In preparing them for decorated creams, they are usually coated with a thin layer of jelly. To do this quickly and satisfactorily it is necessary that the moulds should be quite dry, perfectly cold, and the jelly on the point of setting when put into the mould, which is turned over and over until thinly, but completely, coated. The decoration is a matter of taste; it may consist of pistachio shredded or finely chopped, almonds, glacé cherries, etc., and may afford no indication of the composition of the cream. But just as frequently the decoration consists of fancifully-cut pieces of the fruit which, reduced to a purée, forms the basis of the cream. This branch of cookery affords almost unlimited scope for display of artistic taste. Success in this direction depends largely on a suitable combination of contrasting or harmonising colours, and the decoration being neat and uniformly disposed. Each section of the mould must be decorated separately, and the decoration fixed firmly by means of a little cool jelly, which must be allowed to set before the position of the mould is changed. For this reason the process is a slow one unless the mould meanwhile rests upon and is surrounded by ice. Without this aid the task is almost an impossible one in hot weather.

GELATINE

Gelatine is obtainable in packets, sheets, strips (or shavings), and powder, and the best qualities are entirely free from any unpleasant taste. Of the three forms in which it is sold, the packet is to be preferred, as it dissolves more readily, and although leaf gelatine is mentioned in the following recipes, the packet gelatine may be substituted by the many who prefer it. However, when doing so, rather less than the quantity of leaf must be used, and only 10 to 20 minutes' soaking is needed. It is always best to soak the gelatine first, and then stir it in a small saucepan by the side of the fire in a very small quantity of water until dissolved. A little more is required in summer than in winter, and when the cream or jelly is to be put into one large mould instead of several small moulds.

JELLIES

Jellies may be described as solutions of gelatine in water, with wine, fruit, and other additions, and their clear, brilliant transparency is one of their chief recommendations. However, jellies of this class do not comprise the whole list, for in addition there are the opaque nourishing milk and egg jellies, and also those made of apples and other fruit. Calf's foot jelly, which is stiffened by the gelatine extracted from the feet by boiling, has the advantage of being perfectly pure, but it is not more nourishing than the jelly made from bought gelatine. When nourishing jelly is required, it is better made from good veal stock. For ordinary garnishing and masking purposes, jelly made from leaf gelatine is more frequently employed than that made from meat. A plain lemon jelly answers admirably for coating the moulds for creams; and variously coloured and flavoured, it forms the basis of many other jellies. By adding a little gold and silver leaf or a few drops of yellow, red, or green vegetable colouring matter, considerable variety may be introduced at small cost. Pleasing effects may be produced by filling the projecting divisions of a mould with gold, silver, or coloured jelly, and the body of the mould with jelly that differs either in colour or character. Of course, the colours must be blended artistically; bright-coloured creams, like strawberry, should be very simply decorated; and the creamy-white of the almond or the delicate green of the pistachio nut, embedded in the amber-hued jelly with which the mould is lined, contrast favourably with chocolate, as also does finely-flaked gold leaf.

TO CLEAR JELLY

The agent employed for this purpose is albumen, of which substance the white of egg is largely composed. The shells and lightly-beaten whites of eggs are added to the water, wine, etc., when cold, the whole being continuously whisked while coming to the boil. At a temperature of 160° F., the albumen coagulates, and as the hardened particles rise to the surface they entangle and carry with them all the insoluble substances with which they come in contact; this forms the scum and the filtering medium, through which the jelly must be afterwards passed and repassed until clear. The jelly should always be allowed to simmer for a short time after it reaches boiling-point, but it must on no account be whipped, stirred, or otherwise disturbed. A little lemon-juice or any other acid assists in the coagulation of the albumen.

STRAINING JELLY

For this purpose a jelly-stand and bag are desirable but not indispensable, for an inverted chair and a clean linen cloth may be made to do duty instead. Whichever is used, it must be previously scalded to prevent the jelly setting while running through; and on a cold day, when the jelly runs through slowly, it is advisable to place a basin of hot water in the midst of it to keep it warm. The jelly-bag or cloth must never be squeezed, as a very slight pressure will force through the particles of scum, and make the jelly cloudy.

CREAMS

The term cream is used to describe compounds of cream

and fruit, fruit-purée, etc., or custards, variously flavoured, stiffened with gelatine, and more or less elaborately decorated. For this purpose double cream is required, that is, cream skimmed off milk that has stood for 24 hours instead of 12, or been well-drained from the milk after being separated. Cream is more quickly whipped to a stiff froth when cold, and the air introduced by whipping should be as cold as possible. The process should not be continued one moment after the proper degree of stiffness is obtained, great care being needed in warm weather, when the cream, if over-whipped, is apt to turn rather quickly to butter.   Apart from the manipulation of the cream, an important factor in all preparations of this description of which it forms a part, there are one or two points which need careful attention.   The gelatine, dissolved in a little water, must be added at a certain temperature, for if it be too hot it causes the cream to lose some of its lightness ; if too cold, it sets in small hard lumps instead of being intimately mixed with the whole.   And again, after the gelatine is added, the cream preparation must be stirred until just on the point of setting, more particularly so when it contains fruit, almonds, etc., which would otherwise sink to the bottom of the mould.   On the other hand, if the mixture is allowed to become too cold, it does not take the shape of the mould. If available, the mould should stand on ice until the cream sets.   When creams have to set without this aid, they should be made the day before, and kept in a cold place until required.

TO UNMOULD JELLIES AND CREAMS

It is much better to dip the mould once into hot water than 3 or 4 times into lukewarm water ; and as the whole is immersed it is necessary that the top of the jelly or cream should be afterwards dried with a clean cloth.   One sharp " up and down " jerk will instantly detach the mould of cream or jelly, which should at once be placed on a cold dish, the hand being gently withdrawn.   In turning out a border mould too large to be covered by the hand, the dish and mould together may be shaken sharply up and down.

Sweets of this description are usually garnished with a macédoine of fruit, whipped cream, or jelly.   As a rule the jelly is chopped, and the more coarsely the better is the effect, for large pieces reflect the light, whereas finely-chopped jelly has a slightly opaque appearance.

ICES

Ices may be broadly divided into two classes, viz., cream ices and water ices. The former are sometimes composed almost entirely of cream, sweetened, flavoured and elaborated in a number of ways, but more frequently the so-called "cream ice" consists principally of custard, more or less rich according to respective requirements, with the addition of fruit pulp, crystallized fruit, almonds, chocolate, coffee, liqueurs, and other flavouring ingredients. Water ices are usually prepared from the juices of fresh fruit mixed with syrup, fruit syrup, or jam, sieved and diluted with water or syrup. In addition to these there are the demi-glacé or half-frozen compounds now largely introduced into high-class menus under the names of sorbet, granite or granito, and punch. This variety is always served immediately before the roast, and always in small portions in sorbet cups or glasses, never moulded ; and alcoholic liqueurs are more or less used in their preparation. Parfaits, mousses, and soufflés differ from ordinary ices, inasmuch as the cream preparation is at once moulded and placed on ice, thus omitting the ordinary preliminary freezing process. In these, as in dessert ices, new combinations and moulds of original design are being constantly introduced, but as the principal constituents of the preparations remain unchanged, they present no difficulty to those who understand the general principles.

FREEZING MACHINES

Recent years have introduced a variety of machines for making ices, but the ordinary old-fashioned pewter freezing-pot still holds its own, and deservedly so, for it is reliable and satisfactory in every way, although its use entails a little more labour on the operator, and the process is slower than with the more recently-invented machines. Except in the case of soufflés, a pewter pot and pewter mould for freezing should always be used ; neither copper nor tin should come in contact with the ice. Nearly all the machines in present use are supplied with an outer compartment constructed to hold the ice and salt, and an inner receptacle in which the mixture to be frozen is placed.

FREEZING MIXTURE

The materials usually employed for this purpose are ice and

coarse salt, or freezing-salt, the correct proportions being
1 lb. of salt to 8 or 10 lb. of ice. More salt than this is often
added with a view to making the mixture freeze more quickly,
which it does for a short time, but the large proportion of
salt causes the ice to melt speedily, and the freezing operation
comes to a standstill unless the ice is frequently renewed.
The ice tub or outer compartment of the machine must be
filled with alternate layers of crushed ice and salt.

PREPARATION OF ICES

The mixture to be frozen is placed in the freezing-pot or
inner receptacle of the freezing machine, and the lid firmly
secured. After a short time, a thin coating of ice will have
formed on the sides. This must be scraped down with the
spatula, and well mixed with the liquid contents, and as soon
as another layer has formed it must be dealt with in the same
manner. This is continued until the mixture acquires a
thick creamy consistency, when it is ready for moulding.

To ensure success the following rules should be carefully
observed :

1. Avoid putting warm mixtures into the freezing-pot.

2. Add sweetening ingredients with discretion.

3. Avoid, as much as possible, the use of tin and copper
utensils.

4. Carefully wipe the lid of the freezer before raising it, so
as to prevent any salt getting into the mixture.

MOULDING ICES

The ice, in the semi-solid condition in which it is taken
from the freezing machine, is put into dry moulds, and well
shaken and pressed down in the shape of them. If there is
the least doubt about the lid fitting perfectly, it is better to
seal the opening with a layer of lard, so as effectually to
exclude the salt and ice. In any case the mould should be
wrapped in two or three folds of kitchen paper when the
freezing has to be completed in a pail. One part of salt
should be added to eight parts of ice, and the quantity must
be sufficient completely to surround the mould. It should
be kept covered with ice and salt for 3 or 4 hours, when it will
be ready to unmould. When a charged ice cave is available,
the ice is simply moulded, placed in the cave, and kept there
until sufficiently frozen.

UNMOULDING ICES

Ices should be kept in the moulds, buried in ice, until required. When ready to serve, remove the paper and the lard, when it has been used, dip the mould into cold water, and turn the ice on to a dish in the same way as a jelly or cream.

FREEZING ICE CREAM IN A REFRIGERATOR

Ice cream may be frozen quite satisfactorily in a refrigerator. In order to obtain a good texture and minimize the risk of ice crystals forming within the ice cream, certain points should be taken into consideration.

The quicker the freezing the less likelihood there is of crystal formation, so the indicator should be turned to the lowest possible temperature.

The mixture should be stirred from time to time, or even beaten, during the freezing process.

The presence of air is also a deterrent to crystal formation, as is also the inclusion of a farinaceous substance, so a good result may often be obtained by the use of a stiffly-whipped white of egg or cream, a little cornflour, or allied substance.

CHAPTER II

RECIPES FOR COLD SWEETS

ALMOND CUSTARD.

Measure out 1 tablespoonful of finely-chopped almonds, a few drops of almond-essence, ½ an oz. of potato flour, 4 oz. of castor sugar, 2 or 3 yolks of eggs, 3 sheets or ¼ of an oz. of leaf gelatine and 1½ pints of milk.

Mix the potato flour smoothly with a little milk, boil up the remainder, and pour it over the potato flour, stirring the mixture meanwhile. Replace in the stewpan, simmer gently for about 3 minutes, then add the sugar and yolks of eggs, and stir by the side of the fire until the mixture thickens. Dissolve the gelatine in a little hot water, add it to the custard, and strain. Stir in the almonds, add almond-essence to taste, and use for filling éclairs, cornets, small cakes, etc.

APPLE AND RICE CAKE.

Take 3 or 4 cooking apples, 2 oz. of rice, sugar, vanilla and milk, and prepare some good short crust (p. 87). Sufficient for 4 persons.

Simmer the rice in milk until quite soft and fairly dry, then add sugar and vanilla to taste. Peel, core, and slice the apples. Line a flan-ring with short-crust paste, fill with alternate thin layers of hot rice and uncooked apple, and on top place a thin cover of paste. Seal the edges, bake in a fairly hot oven from 20 to 30 minutes. Dredge thickly with fine sugar and serve as a luncheon or dinner sweet.

APPLE COMPÔTE.

With 1 lb. of Normandy pippins, take 1 oz. of almonds blanched and halved, 8 oz. of castor sugar and 1 pint of water. Sufficient for 6 or 7 persons.

Soak the apples for at least 12 hours in the water, then turn into a stewpan, add the sugar, and simmer gently until tender. Drain, replace the syrup in the stewpan, and boil rapidly until considerably reduced. Arrange the apples in a glass dish, pour the syrup over, garnish with the prepared almonds, and when cold, serve.

APPLE CUSTARD.

To 2 lb. of apples, allow 6 oz. of sugar, 3 eggs and 1 pint of milk. Sufficient for 5 or 6 persons.

Peel, core and slice the apples, stew them with 4 oz. of sugar and 2 or 3 tablespoonfuls of water until tender, then pass through a very fine sieve, or beat to a pulp. Bring the milk nearly to boiling-point, put in the remainder of the sugar and the beaten yolks of eggs, stir and cook gently until the mixture thickens, but do not allow it to boil. Whisk the whites of eggs to a stiff froth, and sweeten with a little castor sugar. Place the apple pulp at the bottom of a pie-dish, pour the custard on top, and cover lightly with the white of egg. Sprinkle the surface liberally with castor sugar, and bake in a moderately cool oven until the méringue hardens and acquires a little colour.

APPLE FOOL.

Prepare 1 pint of apple pulp, and take ⅓ of a pint of stiffly-whipped cream, and sugar to taste. Sufficient for 3 or 4 persons.

Bake or stew the apples, pass them through a fine sieve, sweeten, and stir in the cream. Serve in a glass dish or custard-glasses.

APPLE FROST WITH CREAM.

Take 10 small sour cooking apples, 10 oz. of loaf sugar, castor sugar, ½ a pint of cream, 3 whites of eggs, 1 teaspoonful of lemon-juice, 1 inch of cinnamon, 2 cloves, 10 crystallized cherries and a few strips of angelica. Sufficient for 7 or 8 persons.

Peel and core the apples carefully without breaking. Place the loaf sugar in a stewpan with ½ a pint of water, the sugar, lemon-juice, cloves and cinnamon, and reduce to a syrup, skimming meanwhile. Arrange the apples in a sauté-pan, pour the syrup round, cover with a buttered paper, and bake

COLD SWEETS

1. Charlotte Russe.   2. Trifle.

[*Facing page 16*

1. Eclairs.　　2. Assorted Pastry.　　3. Rice and Apple Gâteau.
4. Gâteau St. Honoré.　　5. Simnel Cake.　　6. Pancakes.
7. Pyramid Cream.　　8. Croquettes of Rice.

gently until tender. Transfer them to a buttered baking-sheet, cover the entire surface lightly with stiffly-whisked sweetened white of egg by means of a pipe and forcing-bag, and dredge well with castor sugar. Bake in a slow oven until the méringue hardens and acquires a little colour, and let them become quite cold. When ready to serve, whip the cream stiffly, stir in 1 dessertspoonful of castor sugar, pile a little in the centre of each apple, dish each one on a little bed of cream, and serve the remainder in the centre of the dish. Decorate each apple with a cherry and strips of angelica, then serve.

APPLE HEDGEHOG.

Have ready 1 dozen sour cooking apples, 5 oz. of moist sugar, castor sugar, 1 oz. of blanched baked almonds, 2 whites of eggs, the finely-grated rind of ½ a lemon and 1 pint of water. Sufficient for 6 or 7 persons.

Peel the apples, core 8 of them carefully, and slice the remainder. Place the 8 whole apples in a stewpan with the moist sugar and water, stew gently until tender, then transfer them carefully to a dish. Put the sliced apples into the stewpan, cook them in the syrup until perfectly soft, and beat them to a pulp. Spread a layer of this pulp on a dish, place the whole apples on the top of it, fill the spaces between them with apple pulp, and cover the surface with the remainder, raising it slightly in the centre, in the form of a dome. Whisk the whites of eggs stiffly, sweeten to taste with castor sugar, and spread lightly over the apples. Insert the strips of almonds uniformly, to represent the back of a hedgehog, and serve.

APPLE SNOW.

With 6 apples, take 6 whites of eggs, 4 or 5 oz. of castor sugar, and the thinly-cut rind of 1 lemon. Sufficient for 5 or 6 persons.

Peel, core and slice the apples, place them in a jar with the sugar, lemon-rind, and 2 tablespoonfuls of water, and stew gently on the stove or in the oven until tender. Pass through a sieve, add more sugar if necessary, and let the pulp become quite cold. Then whisk the whites stiffly, add them to the pulp, and continue the whisking until the mixture stiffens. Serve in custard-glasses or on a glass dish.

C.S.   B

APPLE SNOW. (Another Method.)

To 6 apples, allow 2 whites of eggs, 2 tablespoonfuls of castor sugar, 1 tablespoonful of coarsely-chopped candied peel and the thinly-cut rind of ½ a lemon. Sufficient for 6 or 7 persons.

Peel, core and slice the apples, put them into a stewpan with the water, sugar and lemon-rind. Cook gently until tender, pass through a hair sieve, add the stiffly-whisked whites of eggs, and whisk until the mixture becomes firm. Stir in the candied peel, and serve in small glasses.

APPLE SNOW. (Another Method.)

Procure 2 lb. of sour cooking apples, 4 oz. of castor sugar, the thinly-cut rind of 1 lemon and 2 whites of eggs. Sufficient for 6 or 7 persons.

Peel, core and slice the apples, stew them with 3 table-spoonfuls of water, the lemon-rind and sugar until tender, then pass them through a sieve. Add more sugar if necessary, let the apple pulp become quite cold, and mix lightly in the stiffly-whisked whites of eggs. Serve in jelly-glasses or on a glass dish.

APPLE TRIFLE.

Have ready 2 lb. of sour cooking apples, 6 oz. of sugar, ⅓ of a pint of cream, ½ a pint of Custard (p. 29), 3 sponge cakes, the finely-grated rind of ½ a lemon, glacé cherries and angelica. Sufficient for 6 or 7 persons.

Peel, core, slice the apples, stew them with the lemon-rind, sugar, and 2 tablespoonfuls of water in a jar until tender, and rub through a hair sieve. Cut each sponge cake into 3 or 4 slices, place them in a glass dish, cover with the apple purée, pour over the custard, and let the preparation stand until perfectly cold. Then whip the cream stiffly, spread it lightly over the entire surface, and garnish with halved cherries and strips of angelica.

APPLES AND CREAM.

Take 2 lb. of sour cooking apples, 5 oz. of moist sugar, 1 lemon and ⅓ of a pint of cream. Sufficient for about 6 or 7 persons.

Peel, core and slice the apples, place them in a jar with the thinly-cut rind of the lemon, 2 tablespoonfuls of water and the sugar, and cook on the stove or in the oven until tender. Pass through a hair sieve, add the lemon-juice, and more sugar, if necessary, and ¾ fill custard-glasses with the preparation. Whip the cream stiffly, sweeten to taste, and pile lightly on the top of the apple purée.

APPLES, AUSTRALIAN.

With 1 lb. of good dessert apples, take 6 oz. of sugar, mincemeat, butter, and ½ a pint of water.

Peel the apples and scoop out the cores, but do not cut right through; fill the hollows with mincemeat, butter the bottom of a stewpan, put in the apples, sugar and water, and cook very slowly until the apples are soft and transparent; let them cool, then place in a glass dish and pour over the syrup. Serve with cream or custard. It will be found much easier to keep the apples whole if the saucepan is placed in the oven.

APPLES IN RED JELLY.

To 6 apples, allow 6 oz. of loaf sugar, ½ an oz. of leaf gelatine, 1 pint of boiling water, the thinly-cut rind of 1 lemon, 4 cloves, 1 white of egg, castor sugar, and a few drops of cochineal. Sufficient for 4 or 5 persons.

Peel and core the apples, place them in a stewpan large enough to allow them to stand side by side, pour over them the hot water, in which the loaf sugar has been previously dissolved, and add the lemon-rind and cloves. Cover, and stew very gently until the apples are tender, then remove them, brush the tops of them with white of egg, and sprinkle liberally with castor sugar. Add the gelatine to the contents of the stewpan, stir until dissolved, then strain into a basin, and colour red with cochineal. Place the apples in a deep glass dish, pour the syrup round, and put aside in a cold place until set.

APRICOT COMPÔTE. (*See* Compôte of Fruit, p. 28.)

APRICOT MOULD.

Have ready 1½ pints of milk, 2 oz. of ground rice, 1 oz. of castor sugar, 4 tablespoonfuls of apricot jam, or ½ a gill of apricot pulp, and ½ a gill of cream. Sufficient for 5 or 6 persons.

Bring the milk to boiling-point, sprinkle in the ground rice, and simmer for about 10 minutes. Dilute the jam or pulp with a tablespoonful of hot water, and press it through a sieve or strainer into the stewpan. Add the sugar, and when well mixed, pour the preparation into a wetted border-mould. Let it stand until set, then turn out and pile the stiffly-whipped sweetened cream in the centre.

APRICOT MOULD. (Another Method.).

Take 2 dozen apricots, ½ a pint of Custard Boiled (p. 29), Lemon jelly (p. 55), lemon-juice, castor sugar, ½ an oz. of gelatine, 4 oz. of loaf sugar, and ¼ of a pint of water. Sufficient for 7 or 8 persons.

Halve the apricots and remove the stones. Boil the 4 oz. of loaf sugar in the ¼ of a pint of water to a syrup, put in the apricots, remove 6 halves when partially cooked and the remainder when quite soft, and pass the latter through a fine sieve. Line a mould with jelly (*see* p. 8), and decorate it with the partially-cooked apricots. Dissolve the gelatine in a little hot water. Mix the apricot pulp and custard together, add sugar and lemon-juice to taste, and strain in the gelatine. Mix quickly and thoroughly, turn into the prepared mould, and keep on ice until firm.

APRICOTS AND RICE.

Procure 2 dozen fresh ripe apricots, 3 tablespoonfuls of apricot marmalade, 1 quart of milk, 1 breakfastcupful of rice, 1 breakfastcupful of sugar, 3 eggs, the rind of 1 lemon, and the juice of 2 lemons. Sufficient for 1 large dish.

Simmer the rice and lemon-rind in the milk until the rice is tender, adding more milk if the rice becomes too dry before it is sufficiently cooked. Take out the lemon-rind, stir in 2 tablespoonfuls of sugar and the eggs, and cook gently by the side of the fire for a few minutes longer. Place a jar in the centre of a glass dish, and pile the rice round it, sloping it towards the edge of the dish, and put aside until cold. Strain the lemon-juice over the rest of the sugar, boil the syrup, put in the apricots previously peeled, halved and stoned, and a few of the kernels blanched and shredded, and boil gently until cooked, but not broken. Remove the jar, and place the apricots carefully in the space it occupied, piling them high in the centre, add the apricot marmalade to the syrup, and strain it over the apricots. Garnish with the remainder of the kernels, and serve when quite cold.

APRICOT TRIFLE.

Have ready 1 bottle or tin of apricots, stale sponge cake, ⅓ of a pint of cream, 1 tablespoonful of almonds blanched and shredded, 1 tablespoonful of castor sugar, and 1 table-spoonful of lemon-juice. Sufficient for 6 or 7 persons.

Strain the apricots, and boil the syrup and sugar together for ½ an hour. Cut the sponge cake into ½-inch slices, and stamp them out into rounds a little larger than ½ an apricot. Place them on a dish, pour the syrup over them, and let them soak for 1 hour. Now remove them to the dish in which they will be served, and add ½ an apricot to each piece. Strain the syrup, mix with it the lemon-juice, and pour it over the apricots. Stick the shredded almonds in the apricots, and serve the stiffly-whipped sweetened cream piled in the centre of the dish. Peaches or pineapple may also be used in this manner, the trimmings of the latter being mixed with the cream. For a plain dish, stale bread may replace the sponge cake, and a good custard may be substituted for the cream.

ARROWROOT BLANCMANGE.

With 4 heaped tablespoonfuls of arrowroot, take sugar to taste, 1½ pints of milk, lemon-rind, and vanilla or other flavouring. Sufficient for 4 or 5 persons.

Mix the arrowroot smoothly with a little cold milk, bring the remainder to boiling-point, put in the flavouring ingredient, and infuse for 20 minutes. Strain the milk over the blended arrowroot and stir, replace in the stewpan, sweeten to taste, and boil gently for a few minutes. Rinse the mould with cold water, pour in the mixture, and put aside until set. Serve with stewed fruit, jam, or cold custard sauce.

AUSTRALIAN TRIFLE.

Take 12 bananas, 12 oranges, 4 eggs, sugar, grated coco-nut, ½ a pint of cold boiled custard (*see* p. 29), and 2 oz. of citron peel or a few pistachio kernels. Sufficient for 1 large dish.

Peel the bananas and slice them up; lay them in a deep glass dish; remove the peel, pith and pips from the oranges, slice and lay them over the bananas, sprinkling each layer with sugar (to taste) and grated coco-nut ; let stand in ice for 1 hour, then cover with the cold boiled custard. Whisk the whites of the eggs to a stiff froth with a little sugar, and heap on the top. Blanch and chop the citron peel or pistachio kernels, and sprinkle over. Stand in ice till served.

BANANA AND TAPIOCA SPONGE.

Procure 6 not over-ripe bananas, and take 2 oz. of loaf sugar, 1 gill of water, ½ a lemon, 1 pint of milk, 2 oz. of very fine tapioca, whites of 2 eggs, and sugar to taste. Sufficient for 5 or 6 persons.

Peel and slice the bananas, put them in a stewpan with the sugar and water, and cook for about 10 minutes, then add the strained juice of ½ a lemon, and rub through a hair sieve. Boil up the milk and stir in the tapioca. Sweeten to taste, and cook whilst stirring for about 20 minutes. To this add the banana pulp. Re-heat, and stir or fold in the stiffly-whisked whites of eggs. Stir till nearly cold, then pour into a glass dish, pile up high, and serve cold.

This dish is equally nice if served hot ; some whipped cream, slightly sweetened, served with it makes an excellent accompaniment.

BANANA BLANCMANGE.

Have ready 2 bananas, 1 quart of milk, 2 oz. of cornflour, 2 oz. of castor sugar, 2 yolks of eggs, and ½ a teaspoonful of vanilla essence. Sufficient for 6 or 7 persons.

Mix the cornflour smoothly with a little milk, boil the remainder, add the sugar and blended cornflour, and simmer gently for 5 minutes. Let it cool, add the beaten yolks of eggs, and stir by the side of the fire until they thicken. Now put in the bananas thinly sliced, the vanilla essence, and pour the preparation into a wetted mould.

BANANA CHARLOTTE.

Prepare ½ a pint of banana pulp, and take ¼ of a pint of stiffly-whipped cream, ½ an oz. of gelatine, sugar to taste, and Savoy biscuits or strips of bread and some melted butter. Sufficient for a pint mould.

Obtain the pulp by passing the bananas through a fine sieve. Soak the gelatine in cold water, and stir it over the fire until dissolved. Meanwhile, take a plain soufflé mould, and cover the bottom with a round of bread, previously cut in quarters and dipped into the melted butter. If a pretty dish is desired, the sides of the mould should be lined with rounds of bread, of ¾-inch diameter, arranged overlapping each other ; but as 3 or 4 tiers may be required this method occupies considerable time. It may be more quickly lined with long narrow strips the size of Savoy biscuits ; these may also overlap each other, or they may be laid flat against the tin. Each piece of bread must be dipped into the oiled butter before being used. Mix the banana pulp and cream lightly together, sweeten to taste, add the gelatine, and, when well mixed, turn into the prepared mould.

BANANA CHARTREUSE.

With 6 bananas, take 1 pint of wine jelly, a few pistachio kernels, and 1 gill of cream.

Peel the bananas, and cut them into slices. Have the jelly just liquid, not warm, pour a little of it into a chartreuse or border mould, and put a few of the pistachio kernels, blanched and cut into quarters, at the bottom of the mould. When set, pour on a little more jelly, and lay in slices of banana, each slice lapping a little over the other. Pour in, a spoonful at a time, sufficient jelly to cover the fruit, and when this is set put another layer of bananas the reverse way. Put strips of pistachio kernel between each layer. Cover the fruit with more jelly, and when setting fill up the mould completely with jelly. Allow to set in a cool place, then turn out on a dish, fill the centre with the cream, whipped stiffly, and serve.

BANANA TRIFLE.

To 1 pint of cream, allow ½ a pint of lemon jelly, 6 bananas, ¼ of an oz. of gelatine, 2 tablespoonfuls of apricot jam sieved, a good tablespoonful of almonds, 2 dozen ratafias, 1 small wineglassful of sherry and a few drops of carmine. Sufficient for 1 dish.

↵Pass the bananas through a hair sieve, add the jam, cool liquid jelly and the sherry. Dissolve the gelatine in a tablespoonful of water, mix with the other ingredients, add a few drops of carmine to brighten the colour, and pour into a deep dish. Blanch, shred, bake the almonds brown, and let them become perfectly cold. When ready to serve, whip the cream stiffly, and sweeten to taste with castor sugar. Pile lightly on the top of the jellied preparation, sprinkle the almonds over the entire surface, and garnish the base with ratafias.

BLANCMANGE. (*See* **Arrowroot Blancmange, p. 21; Vanilla Blancmange, p. 47; Cornflour Blancmange, p. 28, etc.**)

BORDER OF FIGS WITH CREAM.

Have ready ½ a lb. of dried figs, 1 oz. of castor sugar, ¼ of an oz. of leaf gelatine, ½ a pint of water, ⅓ of a pint of cream, and the thinly-cut rind of ½ a lemon.

Cut the figs into small pieces, put them into a jar with the water (sherry or claret may replace a little of the water), sugar and lemon-rind, simmer gently on the stove or in the oven until tender, and rub through a fine sieve. Stir in 2 tablespoonfuls of cream, pour the preparation into a mould previously wetted, or lined with jelly, if preferred. When set, turn out and serve, with the stiffly-whipped sweetened cream piled in the centre.

BORDER OF FRUIT.

Take 2 eggs, the weight of 2 eggs in flour, the weight of 2 eggs in sugar, 2 bananas, 1 orange, ¼ of a lb. of grapes, 1 oz. of preserved cherries, 2 oz. of strawberries, ¼ of a pint of water, ½ a lb. of loaf sugar, 1 small glass of liqueur to flavour (optional), the juice of 1 lemon, a few pistachios and ½ a pint of whipped cream. Sufficient for 6 or 7 persons.

Whisk the eggs and sugar to a frothy consistency, and sprinkle the flour in lightly. Bake in a quick oven in greased border-moulds for about 10 minutes. When cooked, turn on a sieve to cool. Boil the sugar and water for about 20 minutes until a thick syrup is obtained, flavour this with lemon-juice and the liqueur (if used). Prepare the fruit and put it into the syrup. Soak the borders of cake with the syrup, pile up the fruit, and force whipped-cream round the edge of the border and on the fruit daintily by means of a bag and rose-pipe. Any fruit may be used, such as raspberries and red-currants. The liqueurs also may be varied. Decorate the dish with blanched pistachios and a few glacé cherries.

BORDER OF PEARS. (*See* **Pears, Border of.**)

BORDER OF PRUNES WITH CREAM.

With 1 lb. of prunes, take ¼ of a lb. of loaf sugar, ½ an oz. of leaf gelatine, 1 gill of cream, 1 glass of claret (optional), the thinly-cut rind of ½ a lemon, 1 inch of (whole) cinnamon and some lemon or wine jelly (pp. 55 and 60). Sufficient for 5 or 6 persons.

Stone the prunes, place them in a jar with the claret (if used), sugar, lemon-rind, cinnamon, and three parts of a pint of water, stand the jar in a saucepan of boiling water or in a cool oven, cook until tender, and rub through a fine sieve. Dissolve the gelatine in a little water and stir it into the purée. Have ready a border-mould lined with wine jelly, pour in the preparation, let it remain until set, then turn out, and serve with the stiffly-whipped sweetened cream piled in the centre.

BOSTON CUP PUDDING.

To 1 teacupful of flour, take 1 teacupful of brown moist sugar, ½ a teacupful of milk, 1 teaspoonful of baking-powder, ½ a teaspoonful of grated lemon-rind, 1½ oz. of butter, 1 egg, and some raspberry jam. Sufficient for 1 dish.

Cream the butter and sugar well together, beat the egg in, then add the lemon-rind and flour, stir in the milk, and lastly the baking-powder. Have ready a buttered Yorkshire pudding-tin, pour in the preparation, and bake from 20 to 25 minutes in a moderately hot oven. When cold, split, spread a good layer of jam between, and serve.

CANNELONS.

Have ready some strips of puff-paste, p. 85, about 16 in. long and 1 in. wide, flour and egg, whipped cream, preserved fruit, and some jam, or jelly.

Wrap the paste round short sticks, which must be previously greased and floured, and brush them over with egg. Bake in a moderately hot oven, and, when cold, fill them with sweetened stiffly-whipped cream, compôte of fruit, or any kind of jam, or jelly.

CARRAGEEN BLANCMANGE.

Measure out 1 teacupful of carrageen (Irish sea-moss), sugar to taste, vanilla-essence to taste, 1 saltspoonful of salt, and 1 quart of milk.

Pick and wash the moss, let it lie in cold water for 15 minutes, then drain well, and tie it loosely in coarse net or muslin. Put it into a double saucepan with the milk and salt, cook until the milk will jelly, when a little is poured on a cold plate, and sweeten to taste. Strain, add vanilla-essence to taste, and pour the preparation into small moulds previously rinsed with cold water.

CHERRY COMPÔTE. (*See* **Compôte of Fruit, p. 28, and Stewed Fruit, p. 43.**)

CHOCOLATE FARINA.

Take 8 oz. of chocolate, 4 oz. of farina (cornflour will serve), 2 oz. of sugar, 1 quart of milk, and vanilla. Sufficient for 4 or 5 persons.

Mix the farina, or cornflour, smoothly with a little milk, heat the remainder, add the sugar and chocolate in small pieces, and stir until dissolved. Pour the boiling milk, etc., over the cornflour, stirring meanwhile, replace in the stewpan, and simmer gently for 10 minutes, stirring continuously. Add vanilla essence to taste, and pour into a mould rinsed with cold water. Unmould the shape when set on to a cold dish, and serve.

CHOCOLATE MOULD.

Procure 4 oz. of chocolate, 1 oz. of castor sugar, 1 oz. of gelatine, 1 pint of milk, and vanilla. Sufficient for 4 or 5 persons.

Soak the gelatine in 1 or 2 tablespoonfuls of milk, and boil the remainder with the chocolate. When perfectly smooth, stir in the sugar and gelatine, add vanilla essence to taste, let the mixture cool a little, then pour into 1 large or several small moulds.

CHOCOLATE MOULD. (Another Method.)

With 2 oz. of chocolate, take 2 oz. of cornflour, 1 oz. of loaf sugar, 1¼ pints of milk, and a few drops of liquid caramel (burnt sugar). Sufficient for 3 or 4 persons.

Mix the cornflour smoothly with a little milk, put the rest into a stewpan with the chocolate grated or broken into small pieces, add the sugar, and simmer until dissolved. Then add the blended cornflour and milk, simmer very gently for about

5 minutes, and deepen the colour by adding a few drops of caramel. Turn the preparation into a wet mould, and let it remain in a cold place until set.

COBURG TRIFLE.

Have ready 6 stale sponge cakes, macaroons, raspberry or apricot jam, $\frac{1}{2}$ a pint of cream, $\frac{1}{4}$ of a pint of Custard (p. 29), 1 small glass of sherry or Marsala (optional), angelica, glacé cherries, and a few almonds blanched and shredded. Sufficient for 1 large dish.

Slice the sponge cakes, spread half of them with jam, and cover with the remainder. Arrange them compactly in a glass dish, pour the wine (if used) over them, place the macaroons on the top in the form of a pyramid, and cover with the custard. Whip the cream stiffly, pile it on lightly, and garnish with strips of angelica and cherries and the almonds. This dish should (if possible) be made at least 1 hour before serving.

COFFEE CUSTARD.

Procure some coffee essence, 2 eggs, $\frac{1}{2}$ a pint of milk, and sugar to taste. Sufficient for 7 or 8 ramakins.

Bring the milk nearly to boiling-point, pour it over the eggs previously beaten, and add sugar and coffee essence to taste. Pour the custard into buttered china ramakin-cases, bake until set, and serve either hot or cold.

Note.—Also see Moka Custard, for filling Éclairs, p. 103.

COFFEE MOULD.

To 1 pint of milk, allow 1 dessertspoonful of coffee essence, $1\frac{1}{2}$ oz. of castor sugar, and $\frac{1}{2}$ an oz. of leaf gelatine. Sufficient for 4 or 5 persons.

Boil the milk, pour it over the gelatine ; when dissolved, stir in the sugar and coffee essence to taste. Stir occasionally until the preparation becomes cold and creamy, then pour into a wetted mould.

COMPÔTE OF APPLES WITH CREAM.

With 1 lb. of sour cooking apples, take 4 oz. of loaf sugar, 1 oz. of vanilla sugar, $\frac{1}{2}$ a pint of cream, $\frac{1}{2}$ a pint of milk, 2 cloves, the thinly-cut rind of $\frac{1}{2}$ a lemon, and 2 yolks of eggs. Sufficient for 5 or 6 persons.

Pare, core and stew the apples with the loaf sugar, cloves, lemon-rind, and a little water until tender, then drain well, and place them in a glass dish. Bring the milk nearly to boiling-point, add the beaten yolks of eggs, stir, and cook slowly until they thicken, then add the vanilla sugar. Stir frequently until the custard is quite cold, then pour it over the apples. Whip the cream stiffly, sweeten to taste with castor sugar, pile lightly on the top of the custard, then serve.

COMPÔTE OF FRUIT.

Take ½ a lb. of loaf sugar, ¼ of a pint of water, and some fruit, either fresh or preserved. Sufficient for 4 or 5 persons.

Dissolve the sugar in the water, boil until well reduced, skimming meanwhile. Immersion for a few minutes is all that is necessary when using preserved fruits ; but fresh fruit must be simmered in the prepared syrup until sufficiently cooked, but not broken. The compôte may be served as a separate sweet or as an accompaniment to plain creams, blancmange, etc.

CORNFLOUR BLANCMANGE.

Have ready 2½ oz. of cornflour, 1 tablespoonful of castor sugar, 2 pints of milk, and bay-leaf or other flavouring. Sufficient for 4 or 5 persons.

Mix the cornflour smoothly with a little milk. Boil the rest of the milk with the bay-leaf. Remove the latter when the milk boils, then stir in the blended cornflour, cook gently for 10 minutes, and pour into a mould previously rinsed with cold water. If using the sugar add it to the milk before boiling. Serve with jam, stewed fruit, or fruit syrup.

CREAM EGGS.

Prepare some vanilla blancmange (the quantities mentioned in recipe for **Vanilla Blancmange,** p. 47), and take 5 eggs. Sufficient for 4 or 5 persons.

Make a small hole at the end of each egg, empty them, and as far as possible keep the yolks separate from the whites. Make the vanilla blancmange as directed, and then whisk the whites of 2 eggs and add them to it. When cool, put it into the eggshells, place them in an upright position on the unbroken end until set, then remove the shells.

CREAM SNOW.

To 1 pint of cream allow the whites of 2 eggs, 1 tablespoonful of castor sugar, vanilla essence, cherries and angelica for decoration, if liked. This quantity should be sufficient for 6 or 7 persons.

Whip the cream and whisk the whites of eggs separately to a stiff froth, then mix them lightly together, add the sugar, and flavour to taste with vanilla. Pile up as high as possible in a glass dish, and, if liked, garnish with cherries and strips of angelica.

CUSTARD BOILED.

With ½ a pint of milk, take 3 yolks of eggs, 1 to 1½ oz. of castor sugar according to taste, lemon-rind, bay-leaf, vanilla-pod or other flavouring, and 2 tablespoonfuls of thick cream. Sufficient for 1 pint of custard.

Rinse a stewpan with cold water to prevent the milk sticking to the bottom. Put in the milk and flavouring ingredient, simmer gently until pleasantly flavoured, and add the sugar. Strain on to the eggs, stirring meanwhile, return to the stewpan and stir by the side of the fire until the mixture thickens. Considerable care is needed to cook custard in this manner without curdling it, and anyone inexperienced should, instead of replacing the preparation in the stewpan, pour it into a jug or double saucepan, place whichever is used in a saucepan of boiling water, and stir until the custard coats the spoon. Add the cream, stir 2 or 3 minutes longer to cook the cream, and let the custard cool, stirring frequently meanwhile.

CUSTARD BOILED. (Another Method.)

Have ready 1 pint of milk, 1 oz. of sugar, 1 teaspoonful of cornflour, 1 egg, and lemon-rind or other flavouring. Sufficient for 1 pint of custard.

Mix the cornflour smoothly with a little milk, simmer the remainder with the lemon-rind until pleasantly flavoured, then strain it on the blended cornflour, stirring meanwhile. Replace in the stewpan, simmer gently for 3 or 4 minutes to cook the cornflour, add the sugar, and let the preparation cool slightly. Beat the egg, add it to the contents of the stewpan, stir by the side of the fire for a few minutes, then let the custard cool.

CUSTARD MOULD.

Take 1 pint of milk, 2 or 3 eggs, 1 oz. of castor sugar, ¾ of an oz. of leaf gelatine, 1 tablespoonful of brandy, and vanilla essence. Sufficient for 4 or 5 persons.

Bring the milk nearly to boiling-point, add the sugar and well-beaten eggs, and stir by the side of the fire until the mixture thickens, but do not let it boil. Pour it on the gelatine in a basin, add the brandy and vanilla, stir until dissolved, then pour into 1 large or several small moulds. Sherry may replace the brandy, or it may be omitted altogether. A little cold jam sauce or fruit syrup served round the dish will be found an improvement.

CUSTARD SAUCE.

To 1 pint of milk, allow 2 eggs, 3 oz. of castor sugar, 1 tablespoonful of brandy, and bay-leaf if liked. Sufficient for about 1 pint of sauce.

Boil the milk and bay-leaf, add the sugar, and cool slightly. Beat the eggs well, pour the milk on to them, and strain into a jug. Have ready a saucepan of boiling water, in which to place the jug, keep stirring until the mixture thickens, but do not allow it to boil, or it will curdle. Stir in the brandy, and serve.

DAMSON COMPÔTE. (*See* **Compôte of Fruit**, p. 28, and **Stewed Fruit**, p. 43.)

DEVONSHIRE JUNKET. (*See* **Junket**, p. 35.)

FIG MOULD.

Procure 1 lb. of figs, 4 oz. of sugar, 1 oz. of leaf gelatine, 1 lemon, and 1 pint of water. Sufficient for 4 or 5 persons.

Cut the figs into small pieces, put them into a stewpan with the water, sugar, the juice and thinly-cut rind of the lemon, and simmer until tender. Dissolve the gelatine in 3 tablespoonfuls of water, add it to the rest of the ingredients, and pour the mixture into a large mould. Serve with whipped cream or a good custard sauce.

FLOATING ISLAND.

With 1 pint of cream sweetened and stiffly whipped, take 2 whites of eggs and 2 or 3 tablespoonfuls of raspberry jam

or red-currant jelly. This quantity should be sufficient for
1 large dish.

Beat up the whites of eggs till stiff, and mix the jam or
jelly lightly. Spread the whipped cream lightly at the bottom
of a glass dish, and drop tablespoonfuls of the egg mixture
on the surface, making each small pile appear as rocky as
possible.

FRUIT BLANCMANGE.

Prepare 1 pint of Cornflour or Ground Rice blancmange
(pp. 28 and 34) and ½ a lb. of stewed fruit. Sufficient for
5 or 6 moulds.

Make the blancmange as directed, and put a good layer at
the bottom of large-sized dariol-moulds. When set, place in
each mould a much smaller dariol, and fill the space between
the two with blancmange. Let the smaller dariols remain
until the blancmange is firm, then remove them, fill the cavity
with stewed fruit, and cover with blancmange. When set,
turn out, and serve with custard or whipped cream.

FRUIT, DRIED (Apples, Apricots, Peaches, etc.).

Have ready some fruit, sugar, lemon-rind, and a few cloves
or some cinnamon to flavour.

The following method is applicable to any of the dried
fruits from California and other countries. Rinse or wash
the fruit in cold water, cover it with fresh cold water, and let
it remain in soak for 10 or 12 hours until well swollen. Turn
both fruit and water into a stewpan or a jar placed in a pan
of boiling water, and cook gently until the fruit is tender.
Sugar to taste, or sugar boiled to a syrup (*see* **Sugar for
Compôtes,** p. 46), and flavouring ingredients should be
added when the fruit is half cooked. When syrup is used
the water required for it should be taken from the vessel
containing the fruit unless a rather liquid compôte is liked.
The water in which the fruit soaks always extracts some of
the flavour of the fruit, and the latter should therefore be
cooked in it. Much stirring should be avoided, as dried fruit,
when nearly cooked, breaks easily.

Newtown pippins, from which the peel and cores have been
removed, and Normandy pippins, from which only the peel
is removed, may require soaking a little more than apple
rings and apple chips.

FRUIT MOULDS.   (*See* **Jelly with Bananas,** p. 54, **Jelly with Fruit,** p. 55, etc.)

FRUIT SALAD.   (*See* **Compôte of Fruit,** p. 28.)

GENEVA WAFERS.

Take 3 oz. of fine flour, 2 oz. of castor sugar, 3 oz. of butter, 2 eggs, vanilla essence, cream, and some apricot jam.   Sufficient for 6 or 7 persons.

Cream the butter and sugar well together, beat each egg in separately, add a few drops of vanilla, and stir the flour in as lightly as possible.   Put the mixture into a forcing-bag with a large plain pipe, force it out on a well-buttered baking-tin in portions that would just fill a teaspoon, and spread out thinly with a hot wet palette-knife.   Bake in a moderate oven until set, then take them out carefully with a palette-knife, and wrap them round buttered cornet tins.   Place one inside the other, to keep them in shape, replace in the oven, and bake until lightly browned, turning them frequently in order that all parts may be equally coloured.   When cool remove the moulds, partly fill them with stiffly-whipped, sweetened cream, add a little jam, and fill the remaining space with cream.

GLAZED APPLES.

Have ready some small apples of equal size, lemon-juice, Syrup (p. 46), apricot jam or marmalade, red-currant jelly, strips of angelica and sugar.

Pare and core the apples, and simmer them very gently in water to which sugar to taste and a little lemon-juice has been added.   Drain well, pour over them a little syrup, and cover closely.   When cold, coat the apples with apricot marmalade, fill the cavities from which the cores were removed with jelly, and decorate tastefully with strips or leaves of angelica.

GOOSEBERRIES, COMPÔTE OF.   (*See* **Compôte of Fruit,** p. 28, and **Stewed Fruit,** p. 43.)

GOOSEBERRY CHARLOTTE.

Prepare some Gooseberry cream (p. 67), and procure some finger biscuits, sponge cake, or Génoise.

Line a plain charlotte-mould with the biscuits or slices of the cake, cutting them to fit both the bottom and sides of the mould. Make the cream as directed; when on the point of setting, turn it into the prepared mould, and set on ice until firm.

GOOSEBERRY FOOL.

With 1 quart of green gooseberries take ¼ of a lb. of loaf sugar, 1 pint of cream and ½ a pint of water. Sufficient for 6 or 7 persons.

Top and tail the gooseberries, cook them until tender with the water and sugar in a jar placed in a saucepan of boiling water. Rub them through a hair sieve, add more sugar if necessary, and let the pulp become quite cold. Whip the cream stiffly, and stir it into the preparation a few minutes before serving. [Custard (p. 29) may be used instead, if preferred.] Send to table in custard-glasses or large dish.

GOOSEBERRY TRIFLE.

To 2 lb. of green gooseberries allow 6 oz. of sugar, ⅓ of a pint of cream, ½ a pint of Custard (p. 29), 3 sponge cakes and 1 oz. of almonds. Sufficient for 6 or 7 persons.

Stew the gooseberries with the sugar and 4 tablespoonfuls of water in a jar until tender, then rub through a fine sieve. Divide each sponge cake into 3 or 4 slices, place them in a deep dish, cover with the gooseberry pulp, pour over the warm custard, and allow the preparation to become perfectly cold. When ready to serve whip the cream stiffly, spread it lightly over the entire surface, sprinkle with almonds previously blanched, shredded and baked golden-brown, and serve.

GREEN FIG COMPÔTE.

Measure out 1 pint of green figs (tinned ones will serve), ½ a lb. of loaf sugar, ¾ of a pint of water, 1 dessertspoonful of lemon-juice, and take the finely-grated rind of 1 lemon. Sufficient for 4 or 5 persons.

Boil the water, sugar and lemon-rind for 20 minutes, add the figs, and simmer very gently until tender. Remove very carefully, add the lemon-juice to the syrup, strain it over the figs, and, when cold, serve. Dried figs may be prepared in the same way.

C.S.   C

GREENGAGES, COMPÔTE OF. (*See* **Compôte of Fruit**, p. 28, and **Stewed Fruit**, p. 43.)

GROUND RICE BLANCMANGE.

Take 1½ oz. of ground rice, 1½ oz. of castor sugar, 1 pint of milk, and vanilla-pod, lemon-rind or other flavouring. Sufficient for 4 or 5 persons.

Mix the ground rice smoothly with a little milk, boil the remainder with the vanilla-pod or lemon-rind, and let it infuse for a few minutes. Strain on to the blended rice, stirring meanwhile ; replace in the stewpan, and simmer gently for 10 minutes. Now add the sugar, and pour into a wet blancmange mould.

ICED FRUIT.

Fruit of nearly every description may be iced by first dipping it in beaten white of egg, and afterwards in crushed loaf sugar, the process being repeated until a sufficiently thick coating is obtained. Pineapples should be sliced ; pears, peaches and plums should be halved after removing the skins ; cherries, strawberries and similar fruit are iced with the stems on ; and from oranges and lemons every particle of pith is removed before dividing the former into sections and the latter into slices (*see also* following recipe which describes another method for **Iced Oranges**).

ICED ORANGES.

Have ready some oranges, icing sugar, and to each lb. allow 2 stiffly-whisked whites of eggs.

Remove the rinds and pith carefully, and pass a thread through the centre of each orange. Beat the sugar and whites of eggs together until quite smooth, dip each orange in separately, and tie them securely to a stick. Place the stick across the oven, which must be very cool, and let them remain until perfectly dry.

If well-coated and smoothed with a palette-knife they have the appearance of balls of snow.

ISINGLASS BLANCMANGE.

Take 1 oz. of patent isinglass, sugar to taste, ½ a pint of cream, 1 pint of milk and 2 or 3 thin strips of lemon-rind. Sufficient for 5 or 6 persons.

Soak the isinglass and lemon-rind in the milk for 2 hours, then simmer gently for 20 minutes. Strain, replace in the stewpan, add the cream, sweeten to taste, and boil up. When cool, turn into a mould that has been previously rinsed with cold water.

JAUNE-MANGE.

With the yolks of 4 eggs take 1 oz. of gelatine, sugar to taste, the thin rind and strained juice of 1 large lemon, a wineglassful of white wine and 1 pint of water. Sufficient for about 1 quart.

Soak the gelatine in the water for ½ an hour, then add the lemon-rind, and simmer gently until the gelatine is dissolved. Strain into a jug containing the yolks of eggs, add the wine and lemon-juice, and sweeten to taste. Place the jug in a saucepan of boiling water, stir until the contents thicken, and, when cool, pour into a mould previously rinsed with cold water.

JUNKET.

To 1 pint of milk take some junket powder, or 1 dessert-spoonful of essence of rennet, and 1 teaspoonful of castor sugar. The amount of junket powder required is stated on the wrapper; its use may be recommended in preference to the liquid essence, which, in consequence of its varying strength, is uncertain in its results. Sufficient for 3 or 4 persons.

Warm the milk (the exact temperature should be 98° F., the natural heat of the milk), put it into the bowl or deep dish in which it will be served, add the sugar, and stir in the rennet or junket powder. Let it remain in a moderately warm place until set.

LEMON BLANCMANGE. (*See* Vanilla Blancmange, p. 47.)

Follow the directions, substituting lemon-rind for the vanilla-pod.

LEMON SPONGE.

To ½ a pint of water allow 1 oz. of castor sugar, ½ an oz. of leaf gelatine, 1 lemon and 1 white of egg. Sufficient for 4 or 5 persons.

Heat the water, sugar, gelatine and thinly-cut lemon-rind together, stir until the gelatine is dissolved, then strain to the white of egg and lemon-juice previously mixed in a large basin. Whisk all together until stiff, then pile on a dish, and, if liked, colour the last portion with carmine or cochineal, and place it on the top. If preferred, the sponge may be set in a mould rinsed with cold water, and turned out when firm.

MACARONI, SWEET.

Have ready ¼ of a lb. of macaroni, 1½ pints of milk, 2 oz. of sugar, the thinly-cut rind of 1 lemon, ¾ of a pint of Custard (p. 29), and nutmeg. Sufficient for 4 or 5 persons.

Boil the milk, add the sugar, lemon-rind, macaroni in 3-inch lengths, and simmer gently until tender, but firm and unbroken. Place the macaroni in a deep dish, let it become quite cold, then pour over the prepared cold custard, grate with nutmeg, and serve.

MACAROON TRIFLE.

Procure 12 or 14 macaroons, 6 ratafias, 1 oz. of castor sugar, 3 oz. of glacé fruits (cherries, etc.), ¼ of an oz. of pistachios, 2 eggs, 1½ gills of milk, 1 gill of cream and 1 small glass of sherry (optional). Sufficient for 6 or 7 persons.

Bring the milk nearly to boiling-point, add the sugar and beaten yolks of eggs, and stir by the side of the fire until the mixture thickens, but do not let it boil, or the eggs may curdle. Place the macaroons compactly in a deep dish, add the crumbled ratafias, and, if used, pour over the sherry. Stir the custard frequently until quite cold, then pour it over the biscuits, pile the stiffly-whipped sweetened cream on the top, and garnish with shredded pistachios and fruits.

MARBLED MOULD.

Have ready some blancmange, coffee essence, cochineal, saffron-yellow and spinach-green.

Prepare the blancmange according to the directions given (see **Cornflour** or **Ground Rice Blancmange**, pp. 28 and 34), divide it into four equal parts, and colour them respectively with coffee essence, cochineal, saffron-yellow and spinach-green. Mould separately, and, when cool, divide in irregularly-shaped pieces about the size of a walnut. Have ready some white blancmange on the point of setting. Place the coloured pieces in a mould, leaving spaces between them, fill these with white blancmange, and put aside in a cool place until set.

MÉRINGUES.

Take 5 whites of eggs and ½ a lb. of castor sugar.

Put the whites of eggs in a bowl or basin with a pinch of salt, and whisk them stiffly. Sieve the sugar, stir in as lightly as possible with a spoon, folding it in, rather than mixing it with, the whites of eggs. Cover a ¾-inch thick board or a baking-tin with foolscap paper (slightly oiled). Put the preparation into a forcing-bag attached to a plain pipe, and press on to the paper small round or oval portions in rows about 1 inch apart. Dredge them well with castor sugar, and bake in a cool oven for about 2 hours, when they should have acquired a pale fawn colour, and be perfectly crisp. Turn them over, scoop out any portion not hardened and let them remain in a warm place until dry. Use as required.

Note.—When a forcing-bag and pipe are not available, the mixture may be shaped in the form of an egg, by means of a spoon and knife first dipped in hot water. Méringue shells may be kept for a considerable time in an air-tight tin box.

MÉRINGUES À LA CHANTILLY.

With 16 méringue cases take ⅓ to ½ a pint of cream, according to the size of the shells, and vanilla sugar.

Prepare the shells as directed in the preceding recipe. Whip the cream stiffly, sweeten to taste with vanilla sugar, place two together, enclosing the cream, and serve.

MILAN SOUFFLÉ.

To ½ a pint of double cream allow ½ an oz. of gelatine, 2 oz. of castor sugar, the yolks of 4 eggs, the juice of 3 lemons and the finely-grated rinds of 2 lemons. Sufficient for 5 or 6 persons.

Whisk the yolks of eggs and sugar in a stewpan over the fire until creamy, but do not let the mixture boil. Stir in the lemon-rind and juice, and put aside till cold. Soak the gelatine in a little cold water, then stir it over the fire until dissolved, and strain. Whip the cream stiffly, add the gelatine, and stir the egg mixture lightly in. Turn into a silver or china soufflé-dish, and place in a charged ice cabinet for about 2 hours, then serve.

NOUGAT CORNETS WITH CREAM.

Have ready ½ a lb. of sweet almonds, ½ a lb. of castor sugar, the juice of ½ a lemon, 1 gill of cream, vanilla sugar and a few pistachios. Sufficient for 6 or 7 persons.

Blanch, shred and bake the almonds pale-brown. Put the sugar and strained lemon-juice into a sugar boiler, cook until golden-brown, and add the prepared almonds. Let the mixture boil up again, then pour on to an oiled slab, and quickly stamp out some rounds about 2½ inches in diameter. Wrap each one quickly round an oiled cornet-mould to keep the cornet in shape. When cold, remove the moulds, fill the cornets with stiffly-whipped sweetened cream, garnish with chopped pistachios, and serve.

ORANGE COMPÔTE. (*See* **Compôte of Fruit, p.** 28.)

ORANGE CUSTARD.

With 4 oranges take 4 oz. of loaf sugar, 3 eggs, ¼ of a pint of cream, and some candied orange-peel. Sufficient for 6 or 7 persons.

Place the sugar, very thinly-cut rinds and juice of the oranges in a basin, and add 1½ pints of boiling water. Let these ingredients remain covered for 2 hours, then strain into a stewpan, and bring nearly to boiling-point. Add the beaten eggs, and stir by the side of the fire until they thicken. When cool, pour into custard-glasses, and when quite cold, pile the stiffly-whipped cream on the top, and garnish with fine strips of candied orange-peel.

ORANGE FLOAT.

To 1 pint of cream, sweetened and stiffly whipped, allow 2 whites of eggs, 3 tablespoonfuls of orange pulp and castor sugar. Sufficient for 1 large dish.

Beat the whites of eggs and orange pulp together until light, and sweeten to taste. Spread the whipped cream lightly at the bottom of a glass dish, and drop spoonfuls of the egg mixture on the surface, making each small pile as rocky as possible.

ORANGE MOULD.

Have ready 4 oranges, about ¾ of a pint of milk, 3 oz. of sugar and ½ an oz. of gelatine. Sufficient for 5 or 6 persons.

Remove the orange-rind as thinly as possible, and cut it into fine strips. Strain the orange-juice, mix with it milk to increase the quantity to exactly 1 pint, and add the gelatine and sugar. Soak for 2 hours, then bring gently to boiling-point, and simmer for 2 or 3 minutes. Add more sugar if necessary, and pour into a wetted mould.

ORANGE SPONGE.

Squeeze out ¾ of a pint of orange juice, and take 2 whites of eggs, sugar to taste, and ½ an oz. of gelatine. Sufficient for 1 dish or large mould.

Soak and afterwards dissolve the gelatine in a little boiling water, add the orange-juice and sweeten to taste. When cold, add the whites of eggs, whisk until light, and either mould or serve piled on a dish (*see* **Lemon Sponge,** p. 35). Raspberry sponge may be made by substituting the strained juice of fresh raspberries for the orange juice.

ORANGES FILLED WITH JELLY.

Have ready some oranges, jelly of 2 or 3 colours, pistachio nuts, angelica and almonds.

The rind of each orange must be shaped in the form of a cup with a narrow handle across the top. Remove half the rind of each orange, except that part which forms the handle, by means of a sharp knife, and scoop out the pulp. When an ornamental dish is required, cut the edge of both cup and handle into points, or some other design. Fill the cups with jelly, decorate the light jelly with pistachio nuts or angelica, and the dark jelly with shredded almonds, or, if preferred, use whipped cream as a garnish.

PEACH COMPÔTE. (*See* **Compôte of Fruit,** p. 28.)

PEARS, BORDER OF.

To 2 lb. of small stewing pears allow ½ a lb. of loaf sugar, 2 oz. of castor sugar, 1 oz. of butter, 3 sponge cakes, 2 whole eggs, 1 yolk of egg, the grated rind of ½ a lemon, 1 inch of cinnamon, 1 gill of milk and carmine or cochineal. Sufficient for 6 or 7 persons.

Peel and halve the pears, carefully remove the cores, place them in a stewpan with syrup made with the loaf sugar, a pint of water, a few drops of carmine, and cook the pears gently for about ½ an hour, or until tender. Remove the pears, reduce the syrup by rapid boiling, and re-heat the pears in it before serving. Meanwhile beat the eggs well, and add the castor sugar, lemon-rind, milk, and a few drops of cochineal. Slice the sponge cakes, place them in a well-buttered border mould, pour in the custard, and bake for about 40 minutes in the oven, in a tin containing boiling water to ½ the depth of the mould. When ready, turn out on to a hot dish, arrange the pears on the sponge cake border, strain the syrup over them and serve either hot or cold.

PRUNE MOULD.

With 1 lb. of prunes take 4 oz. of sugar, 1 oz. of leaf gelatine, 1½ pints of water, 1 lemon and cochineal. Sufficient for 4 or 5 persons.

Split the prunes and remove the stones ; place them in a stewpan with the water, sugar, juice and thinly-cut rind of the lemon, and simmer from 20 to 25 minutes. Melt the gelatine in 1 tablespoonful of water, and mix with the contents of the stewpan, add a few drops of cochineal, and turn into a large mould rinsed with cold water.

QUINCE BLANCMANGE.

Procure 1 lb. of ripe quinces, 6 oz. of castor sugar, ¾ of an oz. of gelatine, ¼ of a pint of double cream and 1 pint of water. Sufficient for 4 or 5 persons.

Peel and core the quinces, simmer them in the water until quite soft and broken, but not reduced to a pulp, then strain through a jelly-bag. Replace the liquor in the pan, add the sugar and the gelatine previously soaked in a little cold water, and stir and boil gently until the gelatine is dissolved. When cool, add the cream, mix well, and turn into a mould rinsed with cold water.

RAISIN CHEESE.

Take 1 lb. of raisins, ¼ of a lb. of castor sugar, a good pinch each of cinnamon and cloves, a few strips of angelica and some candied citron peel. Sufficient for 4 or 5 persons.

Stone the raisins, add the sugar, cinnamon and cloves, and stew for 1½ hours in a jar placed in a saucepan of boiling water. When cool, pour into a glass dish, garnish with strips of angelica and citron, and serve cold.

RASPBERRY SPONGE. (*See* **Orange Sponge**, p. 39.)

RHUBARB AND BANANA AMBER.

To 1 or 2 bundles of forced rhubarb allow 3 or 4 bananas, 4 oz. of castor sugar, 4 oz. of cake-crumbs, 2 eggs and some finely-crushed macaroons. Sufficient for 5 or 6 persons.

Wipe and trim the rhubarb with a damp cloth, and cut the stems into inch lengths. Peel and slice the bananas. Stew them both together with very little water, and sufficient sugar to sweeten, till tender, then rub all through a fine sieve and reduce a little. Next stir in the cake-crumbs and the yolks of eggs. Butter a fireproof baking or pie-dish, and put in the above preparation, then bake in a moderately heated oven for about 20 minutes. Meanwhile whisk up stiffly the whites of eggs, and fold in carefully 2 oz. of castor sugar. Spread this roughly on top of the cooked fruit and besprinkle freely with the crushed macaroons. Return the dish to a fairly hot oven for another 10 or 15 minutes so as to set and slightly brown the surface. Dish up and serve either hot or cold. Gooseberries may be used instead of rhubarb if preferred.

RICE AND CREAM.

Have ready 3 oz. of Carolina rice, 1 pint of milk, ½ a pint of cream, 1 tablespoonful of castor sugar, 2 tablespoonfuls of sherry (if liked) and some glacé cherries. Sufficient for 5 or 6 persons.

Simmer the rice in the milk until tender, drain well on a sieve and let it cool. Whip the cream stiffly, stir in the rice, add the sherry (if used) and sugar, and serve in custard-glasses garnished with strips of cherries.

RICE BLANCMANGE. (*See* **Ground Rice Blancmange,** p. 34, and **Whole Rice Mould,** p. 48.)

RICE BORDER WITH PRUNES.

With 2 dozen French plums or prunes take 2 oz. of Carolina rice, 2 oz. of castor sugar, 1 pint of milk, ½ a gill of cream, 2 yolks of eggs, 2 tablespoonfuls of apricot marmalade or jam, the finely-grated rind of ½ a lemon, glacé cherries, angelica and sugar. Sufficient for 6 or 7 persons.

Simmer the rice in the milk until tender, add the lemon-rind and sugar, let it remain uncovered for a short time for some of the moisture to evaporate, then stir in the yolks of eggs. Press into a well-buttered border-mould, place the mould in the oven in a tin, surround with boiling water, and bake for about ½ an hour. Dilute the apricot marmalade with a little water, sweeten to taste, strain over the moulded rice when cold. Meanwhile stew the plums or prunes (*see* p. 43), remove the stones, press the parts together again, and insert a short strip of angelica in each one to represent a stalk. Pile them in the centre of the rice, and garnish with halved cherries and the whipped cream, using a forcing-bag and rose-pipe.

SAGO SNOW.

Take 2 oz. of sago, 2 pints of milk, 2 oz. of castor sugar, 2 or 3 eggs and vanilla. Sufficient for 4 or 5 persons.

Boil up 1½ pints of milk, sprinkle in the sago, simmer and stir until the mixture becomes clear. Add the sugar, let the mixture cool slightly, then put in the beaten yolks of eggs. Stir by the side of the fire until they thicken, cool a little, add the vanilla, and pour into a deep silver or glass dish. Beat the whites to a stiff froth, add 1 dessertspoonful of castor sugar, drop rough pieces into the rest of the milk, previously brought to boiling-point, and poach for about 1 minute. Drain, and serve on the top of the sago custard.

SNOW EGGS.

Procure 3 eggs, 1 pint of milk, sugar and essence of vanilla. Sufficient for 6 or 7 persons.

Boil up the milk, sweeten to taste, and flavour with vanilla. Whisk the whites of the eggs to a stiff froth, put 1 tablespoonful at a time into the boiling milk, and poach until firm. Turn 2 or 3 times during the process, and as each portion is cooked, drain and place in a glass dish. Beat the yolks of the eggs, add them to the milk, and strain into the jug. Stand the jug in a saucepan of boiling water, and stir the contents until they thicken. Let the custard cool, stirring occasionally meanwhile, then pour over and round the snow eggs, and serve when quite cold.

SNOW PUDDING. (*See* **Lemon Sponge**, p. 35.)

This should be moulded until set, and served with Boiled custard (p. 29).

SPONGE CAKE MOULD.

Have ready some stale sponge cakes, macaroons or ratafias, 1 pint of milk, 1 oz. of castor sugar or to taste, ¼ of an oz. of leaf gelatine, 1 tablespoonful of brandy (if liked), 2 eggs, glacé cherries and vanilla essence.   Sufficient for a medium-sized mould.

Rinse a plain mould with cold water, decorate the bottom with halves or rings of cherries, and about ¾ fill it with broken sponge cakes, macaroons and brandy (if used).   Dissolve the gelatine in the milk, when nearly boiling add the eggs, and stir by the side of the fire until they thicken.   Add the sugar and vanilla essence to taste, and pour into the mould.   Turn out when cold, and serve with a good Custard.

STEWED FIGS.

With 1 lb. of figs take 4 oz. of sugar, the juice of 1 lemon and 1 pint of water.   Sufficient for 3 or 4 persons.

Place the figs, sugar and lemon-juice in a jar, boil the water, and add it to the contents of the jar.   Cover closely, stand the jar in a saucepan of boiling water or in a slow oven, and stew gently from 1½ to 1¾ hours.   Serve with a good Custard sauce (*see* **Recipe**, p. 30).

STEWED FRUIT.

To 1 lb. of fruit allow 4 oz. of sugar and ¼ of a pint of water.   Sufficient for 3 or 4 persons.

Apples and pears intended for stewing should be peeled, quartered and cored.   Gooseberries should have the tops and tails cut off; rhubarb is usually sliced, and if at all old the stringy outer skin is stripped off.   Other fruit, such as cherries and plums, should have the stalks removed, but the stones may be taken out or not, as preferred.   Bring the water and sugar to the boil, add the fruit, and stew very gently until tender.   Or, place the fruit, water and sugar in a jar, stand the jar in a saucepan of boiling water, and cook until tender.

STEWED PRUNES.

Procure 1 lb. of prunes, 4 oz. of sugar, 1 pint of water and 1 teaspoonful of lemon-juice.   Sufficient for 3 or 4 persons.

Rinse the prunes well in cold water, then place them in a basin, add the pint of cold water, and let them soak for at least 6 hours.   When ready, put them into a jar, add the sugar and lemon-juice, place the jar in a saucepan of boiling water or in a slow oven, and stew gently from 1½ to 2 hours.

ST. HONORÉ TRIFLE.

Have ready a round Genoese cake 1 inch in thickness, ⅛ of a pint of sherry, ½ a pint of stiffly-whipped sweetened cream, 2 or 3 whites of eggs stiffly-whisked and sweetened, crushed macaroons or ratafias, glacé cherries and angelica. Sufficient for 6 or 7 persons.

To make the Genoese cake, slightly warm 4 oz. of butter in a clean basin until it is quite easy to beat up with a wooden spoon, then add ¼ lb. of castor sugar and beat to a cream ; next add 2 eggs, one at a time, and a little milk, then mix in 6 oz. of flour. Pour the mixture into a greased baking-tin, and bake in a quick oven for about 10 minutes.

Remove the Genoese cake from the tin as soon as it is baked, and force the white of egg round the edge to form a raised border. Replace in a cool oven until the méringue hardens, but do not allow it to acquire much colour. Place a good layer of macaroons or ratafias on the top of the cake, pour the wine over, taking care not to touch the border, and let it soak for at least 1 hour. Just before serving, pile the cream on the top, and garnish with cherries and strips of angelica.

STRAWBERRY MOUSSE.

With 1 lb. of small ripe strawberries take 1½ pints of clear wine jelly, ½ a pint of cream, ½ oz. of pistachio nuts and angelica for garnish, 1 small glass of Kirsch, a round slice of Genoese cake, 2 tablespoonfuls of apricot marmalade and 1 oz. of castor or vanilla sugar.

Pick the strawberries and rub three parts of them through a fine sieve. Fill 6 or 8 very small fluted dariole moulds with jelly and strawberries (halves or whole fruit), and strips of pistachio nuts ; place them on the ice to set. Incrust a dome-shaped mould in a pan of ice. Mix the strawberry purée with a gill of jelly. Sprinkle over the remainder of strawberries (cut into slices), castor sugar, and the Kirsch ; after a while stir this into the purée, together with a gill of stiffly whipped and sweetened cream. Pour this into the mould set on the ice, and let it set well. Fix a round of Genoese cake on to a dish ; the former should be a little wider than the open part of the dome mould, and the centre should be slightly scooped out to hold the mousse. Mask the cake with apricot marmalade, sprinkle the edge with chopped pistachios. Unmould the mousse and place it in the centre of the dish, cover the surface quickly with whipped and sweetened cream, decorate tastefully, then place the little jellies round the base of the dish, and serve.

STRAWBERRY SALAD, CHILLED.

Take 1 or 2 lb. of strawberries (small forest strawberries are best for this particular dish), castor sugar and about 1 glass of hock or claret.

The preparation is very simple. Pick over the strawberries and put them into a salad bowl a few minutes before serving, then add enough castor sugar to taste, and about a glass of white or red wine (hock or claret). Carefully stir the fruit so as to mix the wine and the sugar, and place on the ice for the purpose of chilling, then turn into a fruit dish. The wine is sometimes replaced by liqueur flavour, such as Kirsch, Maraschino, Curaçoa, Benedictine, etc., but the use of wine is considered better for a strawberry salad.

STRAWBERRIES, JELLIED.

Prepare 1 quart of Lemon or Wine jelly (pp. 55 and 60), and take ½ lb. fine ripe strawberries of even size, angelica and carmine or spinach greening.

Prepare the lemon or wine jelly in the usual way. Keep it as bright as possible, and colour with a few drops of liquid carmine or spinach greening, so as to give it either a pale pink or else a pale pea-green tint. Select fine ripe strawberries of even size, and wipe them carefully with a damp muslin cloth. Remove the stems and insert in their place thin strips of angelica. Place a fancy jelly mould in a basin containing some crushed ice, mask the inside with half-set jelly, and place in rows of strawberries with alternate layers of jelly. Continue thus until the mould is filled. The last layer should of course be jelly. Do not attempt to set a fresh layer of fruit till each layer of jelly is firm, otherwise the effect of the mould when turned out will be disappointing. When firm enough, take up the mould, dip it into lukewarm water for a moment, then wipe it with a cloth and turn out quickly on a cold dish.

SUGAR, TO CLARIFY, FOR COMPÔTES.

Procure 6 lb. of loaf sugar, 1 quart of water and the white of 1 egg.

Dissolve the sugar in the water in a large stewpan, but do not let it become very hot. Beat up the white of egg, pour the warm syrup on to it, and return to the stewpan. When the syrup boils, add ½ a gill of cold water, repeat three times, thus using in all ½ a pint. Now draw the pan aside for about 10 minutes, then strain by means of a jelly-bag or fine muslin, and use as required.

SUGAR VANILLA. (*See* Recipe, p. 104.)

SYLLABUB.

Have ready 10 macaroons, 1 pint of cream, 4 oz. of castor sugar, the juice of 1 lemon, the finely-grated rind of ½ a lemon, 1 small wineglassful of sherry or Madeira, a pinch of ground cinnamon and essence of ratafia. Sufficient for 7 or 8 persons.

Mix the sugar, lemon-juice and rind, cinnamon and wine together in a large basin, add a few drops of essence of ratafia, stir until the sugar is dissolved, then add the cream and whip to a froth. Arrange the macaroons compactly on the bottom of a deep dish, and as the froth is formed on the syllabub skim it off and place it on the biscuits. When the whole of the preparation has been reduced to a froth, stand the dish in a cold place, and let it remain for at least 12 hours before serving.

SYRUP. (*See* Sugar, to Clarify, above.)

TIPSY CAKE.

Take 8 sponge cakes, raspberry jam, 1 pint of Custard (p. 29), 1 glass of sherry, cherries, angelica and almonds. Sufficient for 6 or 7 persons.

Split the cakes, spread on a good layer of jam, replace the halves, arrange them compactly in a dish, giving them as far as possible the appearance of 1 large cake. Pour over the sherry, and let them soak for 1 hour. Make the custard as directed, and, when cool, pour it over. Garnish with cherries, angelica, or baked almonds.

TRIFLE.

Procure 18 Savoy biscuits, 12 ratafias, raspberry jam, ½ a pint of Custard (p. 29), 1 wine glass of sherry (if liked), 2 tablespoonfuls of milk, 1 oz. of shredded almonds, 2 whites of eggs and castor sugar. Sufficient for 6 or 7 persons.

Make the custard as directed, and let it cool. Spread jam on half the biscuits, cover with the others, and arrange them with the ratafias compactly on a glass dish. Mix the sherry (if used) and the milk together, pour the mixture over the biscuits, stick in the shreds of almonds, and let the preparation soak for 1 hour. Then pour over the custard, and pile the stiffly-whisked sweetened whites of eggs on the top.

TRIFLE, RATAFIA.

Have ready 4 sponge cakes, 6 macaroons, 60 ratafias, 2 oz. of almonds (blanched and shredded), the grated rind of ½ a lemon, ½ a pint of Custard (p. 29), ½ a pint of cream, 2 whites of eggs, castor sugar, raspberry or strawberry jam, ¼ of a pint of sherry (or milk), glacé cherries and angelica. Sufficient for 7 or 8 persons.

Make the custard as directed, and let it become quite cold. Cut the sponge cakes into rather thick slices, spread half of them with jam, cover with the remainder, and arrange them alternately with the macaroons and ratafias in a glass dish. Pour over the wine, or milk, adding a little more if necessary to soak them thoroughly, sprinkle on the lemon-rind, add the almonds, and cover with the custard. Mix the cream and whites of eggs together, whip stiffly, sweeten to taste with castor sugar, pile lightly on the top of the custard. Build the ratafias in pyramidal form, fixing them together with sugar boiled to the small crack degree (290° F.), and garnish with almonds in the same way.

Note.—**To Blanch Almonds and Pistachios.**—Cover the nuts with boiling water, let them remain for 6 or 7 minutes, then strain, replace them in the basin, and cover with cold water. When cool, drain well, and remove the skins by pressing each nut between the thumb and forefinger. Dry well on a sieve, and use as required.

VANILLA BLANCMANGE.

With ¾ of a pint of milk take ¼ of a pint of cream, 3 oz. of loaf sugar, 1 oz. of leaf gelatine, 2 yolks of eggs and 2 inches of vanilla-pod. Sufficient for 6 or 7 persons.

Bring the milk, sugar and vanilla-pod to boiling-point, and simmer gently until sufficiently flavoured. Beat the yolks of eggs slightly, strain on to them the boiling milk, stirring vigorously meanwhile, return to the stewpan, and stir by the side of the fire until the mixture thickens. Dissolve the gelatine in a ¼ of a pint of water, add it to the custard, and when cool remove the vanilla-pod, stir in the stiffly-whipped cream. Stand on ice or in a cold place until set.

WHIPPED CREAM.

To ½ a pint of double cream allow 1½ oz. of castor sugar or to taste, 1 dessertspoonful of sherry, 1 dessertspoonful of brandy (the wine and brandy may be omitted) and the juice and finely-grated rind of ½ a lemon. Sufficient for 6 or 7 persons.

Put the sherry, brandy, sugar, lemon-juice and rind into a basin, and stir until the sugar is dissolved. Add the cream, and whip, slowly at first and afterwards more quickly, until firm. Serve as required. Raisin or other sweet wine may replace the sherry and brandy, or an equal quantity of raspberry or strawberry syrup.

WHOLE RICE MOULD.

Take 4 oz. of Carolina rice, 1 quart of milk, 3 oz. of castor sugar and the thinly-cut rind of ½ a lemon. Sufficient for 1 large mould.

Simmer the rice, sugar, lemon-rind and milk together until the rice is perfectly tender and the milk almost absorbed. Remove the lemon-rind, pour the preparation into a wet mould, and, when firm, turn out and serve with jam, stewed fruit or custard sauce.

OVEN TEMPERATURES

Oven.	Temperature.	Will brown a tablespoonful of flour in
Slow oven	270° to 280° F.	5 minutes
Moderate oven . . .	290° to 300° F.	4 „
Hot oven	330° to 350° F.	3 „

CHAPTER III

RECIPES FOR JELLIES

ALMOND CHARLOTTE. (*See* **Charlotte Russe, p. 63.**)

Omit the brandy or sherry and vanilla essence, and add **1** tablespoonful of coarsely-chopped, lightly-browned almonds, and a few drops of almond essence.

AMBER JELLY.

With ¾ of a pint of water take 1 glass of sherry or Marsala (optional), ¼ of a pint of lemon-juice, 6 oz. of loaf sugar, 1 oz. of leaf gelatine, 3 or 4 yolks of eggs and the thinly-cut rind of 1 small lemon. Sufficient for about 1 quart of jelly.

Put all the ingredients into a stewpan, and whisk over low heat until near boiling-point, but do not allow them actually to boil, or the eggs will curdle. Strain through muslin or a fine strainer (*see* p. 10), pour into a mould and place in the cool to set.

APPLE JELLY.

To 1 lb. of apples allow 3 oz. of castor sugar, ½ an oz. of leaf gelatine, 1 lemon and ½ a pint of water. This should be sufficient for 1 medium-sized mould.

Peel and slice the apples, put them into a stewpan with the sugar, water, the juice and thinly-cut rind of the lemon, simmer until tender, and rub through a fine sieve. Melt the gelatine in 2 tablespoonfuls of water, strain, and stir it into the apple preparation, and turn into a prepared mould.

APRICOT JELLY.

Take 18 large apricots, 1½ pints of Syrup (p. 46), 1½ oz. of gelatine and 3 tablespoonfuls of lemon-juice. Sufficient for about 1 quart of jelly.

Remove the stones, and slice the apricots thinly. Make

the syrup as directed, pour it boiling over the apricots, and add the lemon-juice. Soak the gelatine in a little cold water, and, when ready to use, stir it over the fire until dissolved. Allow the apricots to remain covered until nearly cold, then strain through a jelly-bag, stir in the gelatine, and pour into a prepared mould.

BANANA JELLY.

Have ready 6 bananas, 2 oz. of loaf sugar, 2 oz. of leaf gelatine, whites and shells of 3 eggs and 1 glass of sherry.

Wipe the bananas, boil them in their skins in 3 pints of water till reduced to a pulp. Strain twice through a flannel bag. Soak the gelatine in a pint of cold water for 10 minutes, then dissolve on the fire. Now add the banana juice and sugar, and boil all together for about 15 minutes. Add the eggs and shells, whisk, and boil gently till quite clear. Strain through a fine cloth or jelly-bag, and add the wine last. Pour this into one or two moulds, and turn out when set.

BANANA JELLY WITH CREAM.

Prepare 1 pint of lemon or orange jelly, and take 6 bananas, ¼ of a pint or less of cream and ½ an oz. of peeled and finely-chopped pistachio kernels. This should be sufficient for 5 or 6 persons.

Skin the bananas and work them to a pulp. As soon as the jelly is cooling a little, stir in the pulp, then add the cream (which should be whipped lightly), mix well together, and put into a previously-garnished mould. Put the pistachio kernels to set in the bottom of the mould with a little jelly. This when turned out will look like a bed of bright moss.

BRANDY JELLY.

Procure 1 small wineglassful of brandy, 4 oz. of sugar, 1 oz. of leaf gelatine, the thin rind and strained juice of 1 small lemon, the stiffly-whisked whites and crushed shells of 2 eggs, 1 bay-leaf, 2 cloves, 1 blade of mace and 1 pint of cold water. Sufficient for a pint mould.

Put all the ingredients, except the brandy, into a stewpan, whisk gently until on the point of boiling, then draw the pan aside, and let the contents simmer gently for 5 minutes. Strain through a jelly-bag until clear, add the brandy, and pour into a prepared mould.

CALF'S FOOT JELLY.

With 5 pints of cold water take 2 calves' feet, 1 lemon, cloves, bay-leaf and mace, the whites and shells of 2 eggs, ¼ of a pint of sherry (optional). Sufficient for about 1 quart of jelly.

Wash, blanch and divide each foot into 4 or more pieces. Replace in the stewpan, add 5 pints of water ; when boiling skim carefully, add the cloves, bay-leaf and mace, and simmer gently from 5 to 6 hours. Strain, and when cold, carefully remove every particle of fat. Now place the stock, the juice of the lemon and the rind finely pared, the whites and shells of the eggs in the stewpan, whisk over the fire until hot, then add the wine. Bring to the boil, whisking meanwhile. Simmer slowly for 30 minutes, strain, and use.

CHAMPAGNE JELLY.

To 1 pint of water allow ¼ of a pint of champagne, ¼ of a pint of sherry, 6 oz. of loaf sugar, 1¼ oz. of gelatine, the juice and finely-cut rind of 1 lemon, the juice and finely-cut rind of 1 small orange, 2 cloves, 1 inch of cinnamon and the white and shell of 1 egg. Sufficient for 1½ pints of jelly.

Put all these ingredients into a stewpan, and bring to the boil, stirring meanwhile. Simmer for about 10 minutes, strain through a hot jelly-bag or cloth, and pour into a wetted mould.

CLARET JELLY.

Take ¼ of a pint of claret, 1¼ pints of water, ¼ of a pint of lemon-juice, the thinly-cut rind of 2 lemons, 6 oz. of loaf sugar, 1½ oz. of leaf gelatine, whites and shells of 2 eggs and a few drops of cochineal. Sufficient for about 1¾ pints of jelly.

Put all these ingredients into a stewpan, and whisk over the fire until it boils. Simmer for about 10 minutes, then strain through a scalded bag or cloth, add a few drops of cochineal to improve the colour, pour into a wet mould, and put in a cool place to set.

CLARET JELLY, FRENCH.

Have ready 1½ oz. best leaf gelatine, ½ pint claret, 1 pint of water, 4 oz. sugar, 2 lemons, a little cinnamon, a glass of brandy and some whipped cream.

Soak the gelatine for 20 minutes in the claret and water. Add the sugar, the rind and juice of the lemons, and cinnamon. Boil gently, and stir until the whole is dissolved, remove to the corner of the fire and allow it to simmer for 6 minutes. Then strain through a cloth or jelly-bag, adding a glass of brandy, and pour into moulds with hollow centres. Before serving, fill the centres with whipped cream.

COFFEE JELLY.

Prepare ½ a pint of strong clear coffee, and take ½ a pint of water, ½ an oz. (full weight) of leaf gelatine, and sugar to taste. Sufficient for 1 pint of jelly.

Put the water and gelatine into a small stewpan, stir by the side of the fire until dissolved, then pass through a fine strainer into a basin. Add the coffee, sweeten to taste, and turn into a mould previously rinsed with cold water. Turn out when set, and serve.

CRAB APPLE JELLY.

Procure some crab apples, sugar, lemon-juice and gelatine.

Halve the fruit, place it in a preserving pan with cold water barely to cover it, simmer gently until tender, then strain. Replace the liquor in the pan ; to each pint allow 1 lb. of sugar and 1 dessertspoonful of lemon-juice, and simmer gently for about ½ an hour, skimming meanwhile. Measure the liquor ; to each pint allow ½ an oz. of gelatine, dissolve it in a little warm water, and strain and add it to the contents of the preserving pan. Pour into a prepared mould or jelly-glasses, and serve when set. If closely covered the jelly may be kept for a considerable time.

Note.—Also see recipe for **Apple Jelly** (p. 49).

DUTCH FLUMMERY.

With 1 pint of water take 1 oz. of gelatine, castor sugar to taste, 2 eggs, the thinly-pared rind and strained juice of 1 lemon, and 1 small glass of sherry, Madeira, or raisin wine.

Soak the gelatine and lemon-rind in the water for 20 minutes, then simmer gently until the gelatine is dissolved. Beat the eggs, add the wine, lemon-juice, the strained water and gelatine, and sweeten to taste. Stir by the side of the fire until the mixture thickens, then pour into a mould rinsed with cold water, and put aside until set.

GOLDEN JELLY.

Prepare 1 quart of lemon or other clear jelly, and procure 2 to 3 gold leaves. Sufficient for a quart mould.

Break the gold leaves into small pieces, stir them into the jelly when on the point of setting, and pour into a mould as the jelly commences to set.

GOOSEBERRY JELLY.

To 1 lb. of gooseberries allow about 3 oz. of castor sugar, ¾ of an oz. of leaf gelatine, the finely-cut rind of 1 lemon and ½ a pint of water. Sufficient for 1 medium-sized mould.

Cut off the tops and tails of the gooseberries, put them into a stewpan with the sugar, water and lemon-rind, simmer until tender, and rub through a hair sieve. Dissolve the gelatine in 2 tablespoonfuls of cold water, and strain it into the mixture. Turn into a mould previously rinsed with cold water, and put aside in a cold place until set and firm.

GRAPE JELLY.

Have ready 1½ pints of wine jelly or gelatine jelly and some black grapes.

Arrange the grapes and jelly in alternate layers (*see* **Jelly with Oranges,** p. 55), and, if liked, intersperse shredded almonds and strips of pistachio kernels.

ISINGLASS JELLY.

To 1 oz. of patent isinglass allow 5 oz. of loaf sugar, the finely-pared rind and strained juice of 2 lemons, the stiffly-whisked whites and crushed shells of 2 eggs, ½ a pint of sherry, ½ a pint of cold water and 1 pint of boiling water. Sufficient for a quart mould.

Soak the isinglass in the cold water for ½ an hour, then put it into a stewpan with the boiling water, sugar, whites and shells of eggs, thin rind and strained juice of the lemons and the sherry. Whisk the mixture until it boils, let it stand 10 minutes to clear, then strain through a jelly-bag or cloth.

IVORY JELLY.

Procure 4 oz. of ivory dust (to be obtained from first-class grocers), 1 wineglassful of sherry, 1 clove, 1 bay-leaf, 1 blade of mace, sugar to taste, and 1 quart of water. Sufficient for a pint mould.

Put all the ingredients, except the wine and sugar, into a stewpan, and simmer gently until reduced to 1 pint. This will take a considerable time. Strain through a jelly-bag, when cold and set remove the sediment, re-heat the jelly, add the wine and sugar, strain into a mould, and put aside until set.

JELLY IN COLOURS. (*See* **Marbled Jelly**, p. 56.)

JELLY, POLONAISE STYLE.

With 1½ pints of Maraschino jelly (p. 56) take 1 pint of milk, 1 oz. of sugar, ½ an oz. of cornflour, ¼ of an oz. of gelatine, 2 yolks of eggs, 1 tablespoonful of Maraschino and ½ a teaspoonful of vanilla essence. Sufficient for 1 medium-sized mould.

Mix the cornflour smoothly with a little milk, boil the remainder, and add to it the sugar, and the blended cornflour and milk. Stir and boil for 2 or 3 minutes, then add the gelatine previously softened in a little cold water. Simmer gently until it dissolves, and allow the mixture to cool a little. Now add the beaten yolks of eggs, and stir by the side of the fire until they thicken, then strain the preparation into a basin, and stir in the Maraschino and vanilla essence. Pour into a flat-bottomed mould, let it set on ice, and cut into diamond blocks of uniform size. Set these in a fancy border mould in layers with jelly (*see* **Jelly with Fruit**, p. 55), arranging them symmetrically.

JELLY WITH BANANAS.

Take 6 or 8 bananas and 1 pint of Lemon or Wine jelly (pp. 55 and 60). Sufficient for a medium-sized mould.

Remove the skins from the bananas as required, as they so quickly discolour. Cut them into rather thin slices, and arrange them in jelly as directed for **Jelly with Oranges** (p. 55). The greatest care must be taken to have the layers of fruit and the spaces of jelly between them uniform.

JELLY WITH CREAM.

Have ready 1 pint of red jelly (claret or port), ¼ oz. each of preserved ginger, apricots, angelica and cherries, all shredded, ½ an oz. of gelatine and ½ a pint of stiffly-whipped cream. Sufficient for 5 or 6 persons.

Place a deep layer of jelly at the bottom of a plain mould, let it set firmly, put in a small round mould, or tumbler with straight sides, and fill the outer space with cold liquid jelly. When firm, take away the mould or glass ; this may be easily done by filling it for a minute or so with warm water. Dissolve the gelatine in a little hot water, when slightly cooled add it to the cream, stir in the fruits, and turn the whole into the prepared mould.

JELLY WITH FRUIT.

Prepare 1½ pints of Lemon or Wine jelly (pp. 55 and 60), and procure mixed fruit, such as grapes, strawberries, red and white currants, small slices or dice of pineapple, peaches and apricots. Sufficient for a large mould.

Rinse the mould with cold water, place it in a basin or shallow pan of broken ice, cover the bottom with a thin layer of cool jelly, and let it set. Add some of the fruit, contrasting the colours carefully, cover with jelly, and leave it to stiffen. Repeat until the mould is full, taking care that each layer is firmly fixed before adding another. Turn out when set, and serve.

JELLY WITH ORANGES.

Make 1 pint of Lemon or Wine jelly (pp. 55 and 60), and procure 6 Tangerine oranges. Sufficient for a medium-sized mould.

Peel the oranges, remove every particle of pith, and divide them into sections. Cover the bottom of a charlotte-mould with a little cool jelly, let it set, then arrange sections of orange neatly overlapping each other round the mould. Cover with more jelly, let it set, then add another layer of oranges, and repeat until the mould is full.

JELLY WITH RAISINS.

Have ready some Wine or Lemon jelly (pp. 55 and 60) and Valencia raisins stoned.

The raisins may be placed in the jelly according to the directions given in **Jelly with Bananas,** or **Jelly with Fruit.**

LEMON JELLY.

To 1½ pints of water allow ¼ of a pint of lemon-juice, 6 oz. of loaf sugar, the finely-peeled rind of 4 lemons, the whites and shells of 2 eggs and 1½ oz. of leaf gelatine.   Sufficient for 1¾ pints of jelly.

Put the water, lemon-rind and juice, gelatine, sugar, egg-shells, and the slightly-beaten whites together into a stewpan, boil up, whisking meanwhile, simmer for about 10 minutes, then strain through a scalded jelly-bag or linen cloth.

Note.—When the jelly is intended to line or garnish moulds, an extra ¼ oz. of gelatine should be added, especially so in hot weather.

LEMON JELLY.   (Another Method.)

With 1½ pints of water take ½ a pint of lemon-juice, 6 oz. of loaf sugar, 2 oz. of leaf gelatine, the thinly-cut rinds of 4 lemons, 4 cloves, 1 inch of cinnamon and the whites and shells of 2 eggs.   Sufficient for 1¾ pints of jelly.

Put all these ingredients into a stewpan, whisk until they boil, and simmer for about 10 minutes.   Strain through a scalded cloth or bag, and when cool use as required.

LIQUEUR JELLY.   (*See* **Maraschino Jelly,** below.)

MACÉDOINE JELLY.

Take some champagne jelly and any fruit in season.

Whip the jelly on ice, in a large bowl, and mix in it all kinds of fruits that are in season.   Preserved fruits may also be used.

MARASCHINO JELLY.

Have ready 4 tablespoonfuls of Maraschino liqueur, 1½ pints of water, 4 oz. of loaf sugar, 1¼ oz. of leaf gelatine, the juice of 2 lemons and the whites and shells of 2 eggs.   Sufficient for 1½ pints of jelly.

Put all the ingredients except the Maraschino into a stew-pan, and bring to boiling-point, whisking meanwhile.   Simmer gently for a few minutes, then strain, add the Maraschino, and when sufficiently cool pour into a wet mould.

MARBLED JELLY.

Take 1½ pints of lemon or wine jelly, cochineal, and some sap-green or spinach colouring.   Sufficient for about 5 or 6 persons.

Coat a mould with a thin layer of cool jelly, put 3 or 4 tablespoonfuls aside, and divide the remainder into 3 equal portions. Colour one green, one red, and leave the other plain. Let it become firm, then put it into the mould in rough pieces about the size of a large walnut, and set them with a little cool jelly, put aside for the purpose. Let it remain on ice or in a cool place until firm.

NECTARINE JELLY. (*See* **Apricot Jelly,** p. 49.)

NOYEAU JELLY. (*See* **Maraschino Jelly,** p. 56.)

ORANGE JELLY.

To 1 pint of orange-juice (strained) allow 1 pint of boiling water, 2 oz. of loaf sugar, 1¾ oz. of gelatine, the juice of 2 lemons and the thinly-cut rind of 2 oranges. Sufficient for a quart mould.

Put the water, gelatine, sugar and orange-rinds into a stewpan, bring to the boil, and let the mixture stand by the side of the fire for about 10 minutes. Have the strained orange and lemon-juice ready in a basin, add the contents of the stewpan, pouring them through a piece of muslin or a strainer. When cool, pour into a mould rinsed with cold water. This jelly is never cleared, as it spoils the flavour.

PORT WINE JELLY.

With ¼ of a pint of port wine, take ½ a pint of water, 1 oz. of loaf sugar, ½ an oz. of leaf gelatine, 1 tablespoonful of red-currant jelly and a few drops of cochineal. Sufficient for a small mould.

Put the water, sugar, red-currant jelly and gelatine into a stewpan, and stir the ingredients by the side of the fire until dissolved. Add half the wine, a few drops of cochineal to improve the colour, and strain through muslin or jelly-bag. Add the rest of the wine last.

PUNCH JELLY.

Take 1 pint of water, 1 small wineglassful each of rum, sherry, and kirsch, ½ a lb. of loaf sugar, 1½ oz. of leaf gelatine, 2 lemons, 1 egg, ½ an inch of cinnamon and 20 coriander seeds. Sufficient for 1½ pints of jelly.

Put the water and sugar into a stewpan, and boil to a syrup. Add the finely-cut rind of the lemons, the gelatine previously softened in a little cold water, and stir until the latter dissolves. Now put in the lemon-juice, rum, sherry, kirsch, cinnamon and coriander seeds, bring to the boil, and let it cool. Beat up the white and shell of the egg, add the mixture to the contents of the stewpan when sufficiently cool, and whisk by the side of the fire until boiling. Simmer very gently for 10 minutes, then strain through a hot jelly-bag or a cloth until clear, and pour into a mould previously rinsed with cold water.

RASPBERRY JELLY.

Let the raspberries be freshly gathered, quite ripe, and picked from the stalks; put them into a large jar after breaking the fruit a little with a wooden spoon, and place the jar, covered, in a saucepan of boiling water. When the juice is well drawn, which will be from ¾ to 1 hour, strain the fruit through a fine hair sieve or cloth, measure the juice, and to each pint allow ¾ of a lb. of loaf sugar. Put the juice and sugar into a preserving-pan, place it over the fire, and boil gently until the jelly thickens upon a little being poured on a cold plate; carefully remove all the scum as it rises, pour the jelly into prepared moulds and keep on the ice or in a cool place until required. This jelly answers for making raspberry cream, and for flavouring various sweet dishes.

RASPBERRY JELLY. (Another Method.)

This is made in the same way as Strawberry Jelly, except that fine, ripe raspberries are used instead of strawberries.

RED-CURRANT JELLY.

Strip the red currants from the stalks, place the fruit in a saucepan with a little water and simmer for about ½ an hour until all the juice is extracted. Then strain through a jelly-bag or fine cloth into a preserving pan. To each pint add 1 lb. of loaf or preserving sugar, and boil slowly for about ¾ of an hour, skim well. When the jelly is sufficiently boiled, it will set quickly if a little is set on a cold plate. Pour into a prepared mould and set aside in a cool place until ready.

RHUBARB JELLY.

To 1 small bundle of rhubarb allow about 4 oz. of castor sugar, ¾ oz. of leaf gelatine, the finely-cut rind of 1 lemon and ½ a pint of water. Sufficient for a medium-sized mould.

Wipe the rhubarb with a cloth, trim it, and cut it into short lengths, put it into a stewpan with the water, sugar and lemon-rind, simmer until tender, and rub through a hair sieve. Dissolve the gelatine in 2 tablespoonfuls of water, and strain into the rest of the ingredients. Turn into a wetted mould, and keep on ice or in a cold place until set.

RUM JELLY.

Procure $1\frac{1}{2}$ oz. of isinglass, or best leaf gelatine, 2 pints water, 1 lb. loaf sugar, 2 lemons, 2 eggs and a glass of rum.

Soak the isinglass or gelatine in 2 pints of cold water for 20 minutes. Add 1 lb. of loaf sugar, and the juice of 2 lemons strained through muslin to keep out the pips. Gently boil it for 1 minute, and stir until the whole is dissolved. Then add the whisked whites of 2 eggs, remove to the corner of the fire, and let it simmer for 5 or 6 minutes. Strain through a flannel bag until clear, add a glass of the best rum, pour into a mould and set on ice.

SAUTERNE JELLY. (*See* **Champagne Jelly, p. 51.**)

STOCK FOR JELLY. (*See* **Calf's Foot Jelly, p. 51, Lemon Jelly, p. 55, and Wine Jelly, p. 60.**)

STRAWBERRY JELLY.

With 1 lb. of strawberries take $\frac{1}{2}$ a lb. of loaf sugar, 2 oz. of gelatine, the juice of 1 lemon, the whites and shells of 2 eggs and a little Lemon jelly (p. 55). Sufficient for 1 large mould.

Boil the sugar and 1 pint of cold water to a syrup, and when cool, pour it over $\frac{1}{2}$ a lb. of strawberries, previously picked and crushed to a pulp. Cover the basin, and let the fruit remain thus for $\frac{1}{2}$ an hour. Coat a mould thinly with lemon jelly, decorate tastefully with whole strawberries, and fix them firmly in place with a little more jelly (*see* p. 8). Place the gelatine with 1 pint of water in a stewpan ; when dissolved add the strawberry preparation and the lemon-juice. Let the mixture cool, then stir in the whites of the eggs and the shells. Whisk until boiling, and strain through a jelly-bag or cloth until clear. When the preparation is cold and on the point of setting pour it into the prepared mould, and let it remain in a cool place until firm.

TIPPAREE JELLY.

Procure some Tipparee pods (Cape gooseberries), sugar and lemon-juice.

Wipe the pods, cover them with cold water, simmer gently until soft, then drain through a jelly-bag, but do not squeeze the pulp. Measure the liquor; to each pint add 1 lb. of sugar and 1 dessertspoonful of lemon-juice, and simmer gently for $\frac{1}{2}$ an hour, skimming meanwhile. Pour the jelly into prepared moulds, or into jars if not required for immediate use.

WHITE-CURRANT JELLY.

Pick the currants from the stalk, and put them into a jar. Place the jar in a saucepan of boiling water, simmer gently until the juice is extracted, then strain through a jelly-bag or fine cloth into a preserving-pan. To each pint allow from $\frac{3}{4}$ to 1 lb. of preserving sugar, according to taste, and boil gently until the jelly quickly sets, when a little is poured on a cold plate. Turn into prepared moulds and set in a cool place until required.

WINE JELLY.

To 1 quart of water allow $\frac{1}{4}$ of a pint of wine, sherry or Marsala, 4 oz. of loaf sugar, $2\frac{1}{2}$ oz. of leaf gelatine, 1 orange, 1 lemon, $\frac{1}{2}$ an oz. of coriander seed and the whites and shells of 2 eggs. Sufficient for about 1 quart of jelly.

Put the water, sugar, gelatine, the juice and finely-cut rind of the orange and lemon, and the coriander seeds into a stewpan, and let them soak until the gelatine is softened. Whisk the whites and shells of the eggs together, add them to the rest of the ingredients, and whisk over the fire until boiling. Simmer gently for 10 minutes, then strain through a hot jelly-bag or cloth until clear, and pour into a wet mould.

Note.—When the jelly is intended to line or garnish moulds, an extra $\frac{1}{4}$ oz. of gelatine should be added, especially in hot weather.

CHAPTER IV

RECIPES FOR CREAMS

ALMOND CREAM.

Have ready 2 oz. of almonds, ½ a pint of cream, 1 oz. of sugar, ½ an oz. of leaf gelatine and essence of almonds. Sufficient for 1 small cream.

Blanch and skin the almonds, chop them coarsely, and bake in the oven until light-brown. Dissolve the gelatine and sugar in 3 tablespoonfuls of water. Whip the cream stiffly, add the gelatine, etc., the almonds when cold, and mix all lightly together. Pour into a prepared mould, and stand on ice or in a cool place until firmly set.

APRICOT CREAM.

With ½ a pint of apricot purée, take ½ a pint of cream, 1½ oz. of castor sugar, ¾ of an oz. of leaf gelatine, 1 teaspoonful of lemon-juice, ¼ of a pint of apricot syrup and a few drops of cochineal. Sufficient for 1 medium-sized mould.

Tinned or bottled apricots may be used, and the purée is made by passing them through a fine sieve. Whip the cream stiffly, and stir it lightly into the purée. Dissolve the gelatine in a little water and put with the syrup, add the sugar and lemon-juice, and let it cool, then strain into the cream, etc., and add cochineal drop by drop until the desired colour is obtained. Pour the mixture into the prepared mould, and stand on ice or in a cold place until firm.

BANANA CREAM.

Procure 2 bananas, 1 quart of milk, 2 oz. of cornflour, 2 oz. of castor sugar, 2 yolks of eggs and ½ a teaspoonful of vanilla essence.

Mix the cornflour smoothly with a little milk, put the remainder into a stewpan with the sugar, when boiling add

61

the blended cornflour and milk, and boil about 10 minutes. Let the preparation cool a little, then add the beaten yolks of eggs, and stir by the side of the fire until they thicken. Add the vanilla essence, the bananas thinly sliced, and when cool pour into the prepared mould.

BAVARIAN CREAMS.

See **Chocolate Bavaroise** (Bavaroise au Chocolat); **Banana Cream** (Bavaroise de Bananes) and **Peach Cream** (Bavaroise aux Pêches).

BROWN BREAD CREAM.

Have ready 1 pint of cream, ½ a pint of milk, 3 tablespoonfuls of crumbled brown bread, 1 oz. of loaf sugar, ½ an oz. of gelatine, 2 whites and 1 yolk of egg, 1 vanilla pod and ¼ of a teaspoonful of ground cinnamon. Sufficient for 1 large mould.

Simmer the milk and vanilla pod together until pleasantly flavoured, add the sugar, and when dissolved strain on to the beaten eggs, stirring meanwhile. Return to the stewpan, add the gelatine previously soaked in a little water, then put in the cream and stir until the mixture thickens. Have the sieved brown bread and cinnamon ready in a basin, add the milk preparation, stir frequently until cool, then pour into the prepared mould.

CANARY CREAM.

To 1½ pints of milk allow 4 oz. of loaf sugar, ¾ of an oz. of leaf gelatine, 1 lemon and 3 to 4 yolks of eggs. Sufficient for 1 large mould.

Soak the gelatine in a little milk, boil the remainder with the thinly-cut lemon-rind and sugar for a few minutes, add the gelatine, and when dissolved let the mixture cool a little. Now put in the lemon-juice, the beaten yolks of eggs, and stir by the side of the fire until they thicken. Stir the mixture frequently until cool, then pour into a wetted or lined mould.

CARAMEL CREAM.

With 1½ pints of milk take 3 oz. of ground rice, 1 oz. of castor sugar, the thinly-cut rind of 1 lemon and 2 oz. of loaf sugar. Sufficient for 1 medium-sized mould.

Put the loaf sugar into a stewpan with 1 tablespoonful of

cold water, allow it to boil quickly until it becomes dark golden-brown, then pour it into a dry plain mould, which must be turned slowly over and over until the inner surface is completely coated. Add the lemon-rind and castor sugar to the boiling milk, sprinkle in the ground rice, and boil gently for 10 minutes. When ready, remove the lemon-rind, pour the mixture into the prepared mould, and let it remain in a cold place until set.

CHARLOTTE À LA ST. JOSÉ.

Take 4 oz. of preserved pineapple, Savoy biscuits, ½ a pint of cream, ½ a gill of milk, about ½ a pint of Lemon or Wine jelly (pp. 55 and 60), 1 oz. of castor sugar, ½ an oz. of gelatine and 1 tablespoonful of pineapple syrup. Sufficient for 6 or 7 persons.

Line the bottom of an oval charlotte-mould with jelly; when set, decorate it with fancifully-cut pieces of pineapple, and cut the remainder into small dice. Set the decoration with a little jelly, and cover with a layer to the depth of at least ½ an inch. Stand on ice until firm, then line the sides of the mould with Savoy biscuits. Dissolve the gelatine and sugar in the milk, add the pineapple syrup, and let the mixture cool. Whip the cream stiffly, add the pineapple dice, and when cool stir in the gelatine, etc. Pour into the mould, stand on ice until firm, then turn out and serve.

CHARLOTTE RUSSE.

Procure ½ a pint of cream, ¼ of a pint of milk, ¼ of an oz. of leaf gelatine, 1 tablespoonful of brandy or sherry (if liked), 1 dessertspoonful of castor sugar, vanilla essence, Savoy or finger biscuits, jelly, and some cherries, angelica, or other decoration. Sufficient for 1 medium-sized mould.

Cover the bottom of a charlotte-mould thinly with jelly, and when set garnish with strips of angelica and halved cherries. Cover with jelly to the depth of about ½ an inch, let the jelly set, then line the mould with Savoy biscuits. Dissolve the gelatine and sugar in the milk, then strain it and add the brandy and vanilla essence to taste. When cool stir into the stiffly-whipped cream. Pour into the prepared mould, and set on ice or in a cool place until firm.

Note.—If preferred, the bottom of the tin may be lined with biscuits cut to the shape of the mould.

CHARTREUSE OF APPLES.

To 6 small cooking apples allow about 3 oz. of sugar, ½ an oz. of leaf gelatine, 2 oz. of angelica, 1 oz. of glacé cherries, 1 oz. of pistachios, the thinly-cut rind of ½ a lemon, 1 pint of lemon or wine jelly, ½ a gill of cream, 2 cloves and a few drops of carmine or cochineal for colouring purposes. Sufficient for a medium-sized mould.

Peel, core and slice the apples, cook them with the sugar, cloves, lemon-rind, and ½ a pint of water until tender, then rub them through a hair sieve. Dissolve the gelatine in 1 tablespoonful of water, and stir it into the purée. Divide into two equal portions, colour one pink with carmine, add 1 tablespoonful of cream to the other, pour into separate sauté-pans or round shallow tins, and when cold cut into stars, crescents or other shapes. Have ready a plain charlotte-mould coated with jelly, ornament the bottom and sides tastefully with the prepared shapes and fancifully-cut pieces of angelica, and fix them firmly in place with a little cool jelly (*see* p. 8). Place a small mould in the centre of the large one, leaving about 1 inch of space all round ; fill this space with cool jelly, and let it set firmly. Dissolve the trimmings of the coloured and plain preparations separately, add the remainder of the cream stiffly whipped, sweeten to taste, and add to each portion 1 gill of cool jelly Remove the mould from the centre, and fill the cavity with alternate layers of plain and coloured purée, taking care that each layer is firmly set before adding the following one, and dividing them by a liberal sprinkling of shredded cherries and pistachios. Let the mould remain on ice for about 2 hours, then turn out, and serve.

CHESTNUT CREAM.

With 1 lb. of chestnuts take 1½ pints of milk, ½ a pint of cream, 4 oz. of castor sugar, ¾ of an oz. of gelatine, 2 or 3 yolks of eggs, the thinly-cut rind of 1 lemon, a vanilla pod, 1 tablespoonful of Maraschino, and a few drops of cochineal. Sufficient for 1 medium-sized mould.

Shell, parboil and skin the chestnuts, put them into a stewpan with 1 pint of milk, the lemon-rind and vanilla pod, simmer until tender, then rub through a fine sieve. Dissolve the sugar and gelatine in the remaining ½ pint of milk, cool slightly, then add the yolks of eggs, and stir by the side of the fire until they thicken. When cool, mix with the purée, add the Maraschino, thickly-whipped cream, and the cochineal drop by drop, until a pale pink colour is obtained. Pour into a decorated mould, and let it remain on ice or in a cool place until set.

CHOCOLATE BAVAROISE.

Have ready 4 oz. of chocolate, 3 oz. of sugar, ½ an oz. of leaf gelatine, 1 tablespoonful of crème de riz or ground rice, 3 or 4 yolks of eggs, 1 quart of milk and 1 teaspoonful of vanilla essence. Sufficient for 1 large mould.

Soak the gelatine in a little milk, mix the crème de riz smoothly with milk, put the remainder into a stewpan with the chocolate and sugar, bring to the boil, add the crème de riz, and simmer for about 10 minutes. Let the mixture cool a little, add the beaten yolks of eggs, and stir by the side of the fire until they thicken. Add the vanilla and gelatine, and, when cool, pour into the mould, which may be simply wetted, or lined with jelly, and decorated to taste (*see* instructions on p. 8).

CHOCOLATE CREAM.

Take 4 oz. of chocolate, 2 oz. of castor sugar, ¾ of an oz. of leaf gelatine, 2 yolks of eggs, ¼ of a pint of cream, ¼ of a pint of milk and 1 teaspoonful of vanilla essence. Sufficient for a medium-sized mould.

Simmer the milk and chocolate together until smoothly mixed, let it cool slightly, then add the yolks of eggs and stir until they thicken, but the mixture must not boil or the eggs may curdle. Dissolve the gelatine in 1 tablespoonful of water, strain it into the custard, and add the vanilla essence. Whip the cream stiffly, stir it lightly into the custard, turn into a prepared mould, and stand on ice or in a cool place until firmly set.

COFFEE CREAM.

Procure ½ a pint of cream, ½ a pint of milk, coffee essence, 2½ oz. of castor sugar, ¾ of an oz. of gelatine and the yolks of 2 eggs. Sufficient for a medium-sized mould.

Beat the yolks of eggs, add them to the milk when nearly boiling, stir until they thicken, then put in the sugar and cool slightly. Now dissolve the gelatine in 1 tablespoonful

C.S.   E

of water, and add it to the custard. Whip the cream stiffly, stir it into the custard when nearly cold, add the coffee essence, and pour into the prepared mould. Let the mould remain on ice or in a cold place until firm.

CUSTARD CREAM.

To 1 pint of milk allow 2 eggs, ¼ of an oz. of gelatine, 1 dessertspoonful of sugar, a few drops of almond or vanilla flavouring and ½ a gill of cream. Sufficient for about 4 or 5 persons.

Make a boiled custard in the usual way (p. 29), adding the cream afterwards. Dissolve the gelatine according to the directions, and strain whilst hot (not boiling) into the hot custard. Stir well, and pour immediately into a mould previously rinsed out with cold water. Set aside in a cool place, and unmould when required for table.

GARIBALDI CREAM.

Prepare equal quantities of Pistachio, Strawberry, and Vanilla cream (pp. 69, 71 and 74) and some plain jelly. Sufficient for a medium-sized mould.

Place a layer of strawberry cream at the bottom of a mould, previously lined with jelly, or rinsed with cold water. Allow it to set, add an equal depth of vanilla cream, and when firm, pour over it the pistachio cream. Let it remain on ice until set, and unmould.

GENOESE CREAM.

With ½ a pint of milk take ¼ of a pint of cream, 2 oz. of macaroons, 2 oz. of castor sugar, 1 oz. of mixed glacé fruit shredded, ½ an oz. of leaf gelatine, 2 yolks of eggs, the finely-cut rind of ½ an orange and 1 tablespoonful of brandy. Sufficient for a medium-sized mould.

Crush the macaroons and sprinkle the brandy over them. Put the milk, sugar and orange-rind into a stewpan, boil up, and simmer for 10 minutes, then add the gelatine, the beaten yolks of eggs, and stir by the side of the fire until they thicken and the gelatine is dissolved. Strain over the macaroons and brandy, add the prepared fruit, and when cool stir in the stiffly-whipped cream. Continue the stirring until the mixture is on the point of setting, then turn into the prepared mould. Let it remain on ice or in a cool place until set and quite firm.

GINGER CREAM.

Have ready ½ a pint of cream, ¼ of a pint of milk, 2 table-spoonfuls of ginger syrup, 1 tablespoonful of castor sugar, 2 oz. of preserved ginger, ¾ of an oz. of leaf gelatine and the yolks of 2 eggs. This should be sufficient for a medium-sized mould.

Beat the yolks of eggs, add them to the milk when nearly boiling, stir until they thicken, add the sugar, and set aside to cool. Dissolve the gelatine in a tablespoonful of water, mix with it the ginger syrup, the ginger cut into dice, and pour into the custard. Whip the cream stiffly, and when cool stir it lightly into the custard. Turn into the prepared mould, and stand on ice or in a cold place until required for table.

GOOSEBERRY CREAM.

Prepare ½ a pint of gooseberry purée, and take 1 teaspoonful of lemon-juice, sugar, Vanilla cream (p. 74) and some spinach greening. Sufficient for 6 or 7 persons.

Cook the gooseberries in a stew-jar until tender, pass them through a hair sieve, and sweeten to taste. Make the cream as directed, but omit the vanilla flavouring. Add to it the gooseberry purée with a few drops of spinach colouring, and pour into a prepared mould.

HONEYCOMB CREAM.

To 1 quart of milk allow 1 oz. of castor sugar, ½ an oz. of gelatine, 3 eggs and vanilla to taste. Sufficient for a large mould.

Dissolve the gelatine in a little hot water. Beat the yolks of the eggs until light, and whisk the whites to a stiff froth. Boil the milk, stir in the sugar, add the yolks of eggs and dissolved gelatine, and boil up. Stir in the whites of eggs as lightly as possible, add vanilla to taste, and turn into a mould previously rinsed with cold water. Turn out when firm, and serve with Compôte of fruit or Boiled custard (*see* recipes, pp. 28 and 29).

ITALIAN CREAM.

Take ½ a pint of cream ½ a pint of milk, 1 oz. of gelatine, sugar to taste, yolks of 3 eggs, thin rind and strained juice of 1 lemon. Sufficient for 5 or 6 persons.

Soak the gelatine in a little cold water for $\frac{1}{2}$ an hour, and afterwards stir it over the fire until dissolved. Boil up the milk, infuse the lemon-rind for 20 minutes, then add the gelatine, yolks of eggs, lemon-juice, and sugar to taste. Stir by the side of the fire until the mixture thickens, then strain, and, when cool, stir in the stiffly-whipped cream. The preparation may be turned into a mould to set, or it may be at once served in a glass dish or jelly-glasses.

LEMON CREAM.

With 1 pint of cream take 2 tablespoonfuls of lemon-juice, 1 oz. of ground almonds, 1 oz. of castor sugar and 1 teaspoonful of finely-grated lemon-rind. Sufficient to fill 12 small glasses.

Whip the cream stiffly, adding the rest of the ingredients gradually, and sweeten to taste. Serve in jelly-glasses. For a moulded cream *see* **Vanilla Cream** (p. 74), and substitute lemon-juice for vanilla.

Note.—If liked, a small glass of sherry can be added to improve the flavour of this cream.

NOYEAU CREAM.

Procure $1\frac{1}{2}$ pints of cream, $1\frac{1}{2}$ oz. of gelatine, 1 tablespoonful of lemon-juice, 2 tablespoonfuls of noyeau and 1 tablespoonful of sugar. Sufficient for 1 large mould.

Soak and afterwards dissolve the gelatine in a little water. Add the noyeau, lemon-juice, sugar, and the cream slightly-whipped. Whisk gently until light, then turn into a mould and set aside the preparation until it becomes firm.

ORANGE CREAM.

Have ready 1 good orange, 2 tablespoonfuls of apricot marmalade and some Vanilla cream (p. 74).

Make the cream as directed, but omit the vanilla flavouring, add the strained juice of the orange, the rind finely grated, and the marmalade well reduced. Pour into a prepared mould, and place on ice until set.

PEACH CREAM.

Prepare $\frac{1}{2}$ a pint of peach purée, and take $\frac{1}{2}$ a pint of cream, 1 oz. of castor sugar, 1 gill of apricot syrup and $\frac{1}{2}$ an oz. of leaf gelatine. Sufficient for 1 medium-sized mould.

Pass sufficient peaches through a hair sieve to make the purée. Dissolve the gelatine in the syrup, add the sugar and purée, and stir in the stiffly-whipped cream. Turn into the prepared mould, and let it remain on ice or in a cold place until set.

PINEAPPLE CREAM.

Take ½ a pint of cream, 1 gill of water, ⅓ of a pint of pine-apple purée, 2 good tablespoonfuls of pineapple cut into dice, 1½ oz. of castor sugar, ½ an oz. of leaf gelatine and 1 teaspoon-ful of lemon-juice. This should be sufficient for 1 medium-sized mould.

Whip the cream stiffly, stir it lightly into the pineapple purée, and add the pineapple dice. Dissolve the gelatine and sugar in the water, add the lemon-juice, and when sufficiently cool, stir it lightly into the cream and pineapple mixture. Pour into the prepared mould, and set on ice or in a cold place until firm.

PISTACHIO CREAM.

To 1 pint of cream, allow 4 oz. of pistachio nuts, 2 oz. of castor sugar, 1 oz. of leaf gelatine and a little sap-green liquid colouring. Sufficient for 1 medium-sized mould.

Blanch, skin and chop the pistachios finely. Dissolve the gelatine and sugar in 3 tablespoonfuls of water. Whip the cream stiffly, add the gelatine when cool, the pistachios, and sap-green drop by drop until the desired colour is obtained. Pour into a decorated mould (*see* instructions for preparing moulds, p. 8), and let it remain in a cold place until firmly set.

RASPBERRY CREAM.

With 1 pint of cream take ¼ of a pint of milk, 1½ oz. of castor sugar, ½ an oz. of gelatine, the juice of 1 lemon, ¼ of a pint of raspberry syrup, or 2 tablespoonfuls of raspberry jam, and a few drops of cochineal. Sufficient for 1 medium-sized mould.

When raspberry jam is used instead of syrup, pass it through a hair sieve, dilute with water to make the required quantity, and add a few drops of cochineal. Dissolve the gelatine and sugar in the milk, add the lemon-juice, mix with the raspberry syrup, and stir in the stiffly-whipped cream.

RHUBARB AND BANANA FOOL.

Have ready 5 or 6 bananas, ½ a pint of stewed rhubarb purée or pulp, about 1 gill of cream, or custard may be used if preferred, cochineal, and sugar to taste. Sufficient for 5 persons.

Peel the bananas, and rub them through a fine sieve. Add to this the rhubarb purée, and the cream or custard. Sweeten to taste, and colour with a little cochineal. Serve in a glass bowl or in custard-glasses. Decorate the surface with whipped cream and thin slices of bananas.

RICE À L'IMPÉRATRICE.

Take 2 oz. of Caroline rice, 4 oz. of castor sugar, ¼ of an oz. of leaf gelatine, 1 pint of milk, ½ a pint of cream, vanilla or other flavouring, and some compôte of fruit (p. 28). Sufficient for 1 medium-sized mould.

Simmer the rice in the milk until perfectly tender, and when the milk is nearly absorbed, stir frequently to prevent the rice sticking to the bottom of the pan. Melt the gelatine in 1 or 2 tablespoonfuls of water, stir it into the rice with the sugar and flavouring ingredient, and when sufficiently cool add the stiffly-whipped cream. Turn into a decorated border-mould, and allow it to remain on ice or in a cold place until set. Serve the compôte of fruit piled up as high as possible in the centre.

RICE CREAM.

To 1 pint of milk allow ½ a pint of cream, 2 oz. of ground rice, 2 oz. of castor sugar, ½ an oz. of gelatine and some vanilla or other flavouring. Sufficient for 1 medium-sized mould.

Bring the milk and sugar to boiling-point, sprinkle in the rice, and simmer gently for about 20 minutes. Dissolve the gelatine in 1 tablespoonful of water, add it to the rice, flavour to taste with vanilla essence, and when cool, mix in as lightly as possible the stiffly-whipped cream. Pour into prepared mould, and set aside until firm.

RUM CREAM.

Have at hand 1 wineglassful of rum, 2 oz. of sugar, ¼ of an oz. of gelatine, 2 yolks of eggs, ½ a pint of milk and 1 bay-leaf. Sufficient for 4 or 5 persons.

Bring the milk to boiling-point, put in the bay-leaf, and infuse for 20 minutes. Add the sugar and yolks of eggs, stir until the mixture thickens, then put in the gelatine previously dissolved in a little hot water, and remove the bay-leaf. Add the rum, stir occasionally until cool, and pour into a mould rinsed with cold water.

SEMOLINA CREAM.

Procure 1 oz. of semolina, 1¼ pints of milk, ½ an oz. of gelatine, sugar and flavouring to taste.

Soak the semolina in a ¼ of a pint of milk for 1 hour, then put it into a stewpan with another ½ a pint of milk, and simmer gently for about ½ an hour. Boil the remaining ½ pint of milk, pour it over the gelatine, and stir until it is dissolved. Mix this with the semolina, sweeten and flavour to taste, stir until the cream is beginning to set, and pour into a wet mould. Turn out when set.

SOLID CREAM.

With 1 pint of double cream, take castor sugar to taste, 1 dessertspoonful of lemon-juice and 2 tablespoonfuls of brandy (optional). Sufficient for 5 or 6 persons.

Whip the cream stiffly, add the lemon-juice and brandy (if used), and sweeten to taste. Serve in jelly-glasses.

STONE CREAM.

To 1 pint of milk allow 2 oz. of sugar, 1 heaped-up table-spoonful of arrowroot, 3 drops each of essence of cloves and almonds, jam, strips of angelica and a few glacé cherries. Sufficient for 4 or 5 persons.

Place a good layer of jam at the bottom of a glass dish. Mix the arrowroot smoothly with a little cold milk, boil the remainder, pour it over the arrowroot, stirring meanwhile. Replace in the stewpan, add the sugar, simmer gently for 2 or 3 minutes, and stir in the flavourings. Stir the mixture occasionally until nearly cold, then pour it over the jam, and garnish with angelica and cherries.

STRAWBERRY CREAM.

Take 1 lb. of strawberries, ½ a pint of cream, 3 oz. of castor sugar, ¾ of an oz. of leaf gelatine, and the juice of 1 lemon. Sufficient for a medium-sized mould.

Pick the strawberries and pass them through a fine hair sieve. Dissolve the gelatine and sugar in 2 tablespoonfuls of water, and add the lemon-juice. Strain the gelatine, etc., into the strawberry purée, add the cream well-whipped, mix lightly together, and pour into the prepared mould. Set on ice or in a cold place until firm.

STRAWBERRY CREAMS, SMALL.

With 1 lb. of ripe strawberries take 1 pint of Lemon or Wine jelly (pp. 55 and 60), 1 tablespoonful of Maraschino, ½ an oz. of leaf gelatine, 1 oz. of castor sugar, 2 oz. of loaf sugar, 2 eggs, and some angelica. Sufficient for about 10 small moulds.

Line the moulds with jelly, and decorate them with leaves of angelica and halved strawberries (*see* p. 8). Boil the loaf sugar and 1 gill of cold water to a syrup. Pass the remainder of the strawberries through a fine sieve, place in a large basin with the syrup, sugar, Maraschino, beaten eggs, gelatine dissolved in 1 tablespoonful of water, and whisk over a saucepan of boiling water until the mixture thickens. Now stand the basin on ice or on a cold slab, stir frequently until on the point of setting, then pour into the prepared moulds, and let set.

Note.—As the mixture is poured less quickly into small moulds than into one large one, it should not be allowed to come quite so near setting-point. If, however, it stiffens during the process of filling the moulds, it should be slightly re-heated over a saucepan of hot water.

SWISS CREAM.

Procure ½ a pint of cream, ½ a pint of milk, 1 small glass of sherry, 1 oz. of castor sugar, 1 tablespoonful of cornflour, 1 lemon, 1 teaspoonful of finely-chopped pistachios and some sponge cake. Sufficient for 1 medium-sized dish.

Cut the cake into 1-inch thick slices, place them in a deep silver or glass dish, and pour over the sherry. Mix the cornflour smoothly with a little milk, boil the remainder with the thinly-cut lemon-rind and sugar until pleasantly flavoured, remove the lemon-rind, then add the blended cornflour and milk, boil for 2 or 3 minutes, and let the mixture cool. Whip the cream slightly, add it and the lemon-juice to the cornflour preparation, and pour over the sponge cake. Sprinkle with the pistachios, and serve when perfectly cold.

TAPIOCA CREAM.

Take 1½ oz. of finely-crushed tapioca (sold in packets), 2 oz. of castor sugar, 1 quart of milk, 2 tablespoonfuls of thick cream, 2 or 3 yolks of eggs, the thinly-cut rind of ½ a lemon, 1 bay-leaf, ½ a small pot of red-currant jelly and an equal quantity of lemon or wine jelly (pp. 55 and 60). Sufficient for 1 large mould.

Mix and dissolve the jellies, and when cool pour the preparation on the bottom of a border-mould, and let it set. Bring the milk, bay-leaf and lemon-rind to the boil, and sprinkle in the tapioca. Cook gently for about ½ an hour, then add the sugar, beaten yolks of eggs, and stir until the mixture thickens. Remove the bay-leaf and lemon-rind, and when cool stir in the stiffly-whipped cream, and pour the mixture into the prepared mould.

TEA CREAM.

With 1 oz. of good tea take ¾ of an oz. of gelatine, ½ a pint of milk, ½ a pint of cream and sugar to taste. Sufficient for 4 or 5 persons.

Bring the milk to boiling-point, pour it over the tea, let it infuse for 20 minutes, then strain and add half the cream. Dissolve the gelatine in a little boiling water, strain it into the cream, and sweeten to taste. Whip the remainder of the cream stiffly, stir it into the tea, etc., when sufficiently cool. Pour into a mould rinsed with cold water, and let set.

VANILLA CREAM.

To 1½ pints of milk allow ¼ of a pint of cream, 1½ oz. of castor sugar, ½ an oz. of gelatine, 2 or 3 yolks of eggs, 1 tablespoonful of brandy (optional), and 2 teaspoonfuls of vanilla essence. Sufficient for a large mould.

Beat the yolks of eggs, add them to the milk when nearly boiling, stir until they thicken, put in the sugar, and let the preparation cool. Dissolve the gelatine in 1 tablespoonful of water, and add it with the brandy (if used) and vanilla essence to the rest of the ingredients. Whip the cream slightly, stir it lightly into the preparation when cool, and pour into the prepared mould.

Note.—An easy way to test milk is to put a bright steel knitting-needle into it ; if, on withdrawal, the milk adheres and drops off slowly, it is pure ; if it runs off quickly, leaving the needle bright, it has been adulterated with water.

VANILLA CREAM. (Another Method.)

Have ready ¾ of a pint of milk, ¼ of a pint of cream, 1 oz. of castor sugar, ½ an oz. of gelatine, 1 gill of water and 1 teaspoonful of vanilla essence. Sufficient for 1 medium-sized mould.

Whip the cream, and mix gradually with the milk, add the castor sugar and vanilla essence. Dissolve the gelatine in the water, when cool strain into the cream, mix well, and pour into the prepared mould. Let it remain on ice or in a cold place until set.

VELVET CREAM.

Take ½ a pint of cream, ½ a gill of water, 1 small wineglassful of sherry (optional), 1 oz. of castor sugar, and ½ an oz. of leaf gelatine. Sufficient for 1 small mould.

Dissolve the gelatine and sugar in the water, and add the sherry (if used). Whip the cream stiffly, add to the rest of the ingredients when cool, and mix well. Pour into the prepared mould, and let it stand on ice or in a cold place until it is set.

WHIPPED CREAM. (*See* Recipe, p. 48.)

PYRAMID CREAM.

The pyramid cream illustrated consists merely of coffee cream, p. 65, raspberry cream, p. 69, and lemon cream, p. 68, made in graded moulds and placed one on top of the other. Creams of other colours may be used in the same way.

CHAPTER V

COLD PUDDINGS

In this chapter we include a number of recipes for puddings, most of which are equally nice served hot or cold. Full instructions for preparing the various crusts will be found in Chapter VI.

RECIPES FOR PUDDINGS

ALMOND PUDDING, BAKED.

Procure 1 small roll, 2 oz. of ground almonds, 1 oz. of butter, 1 oz. of castor sugar, 1 pint of milk, 2 eggs, the grated rind of 1 lemon, and a good pinch of cinnamon. Sufficient for 5 or 6 persons.

Butter a pie-dish and line the bottom with thin, buttered slices of roll. Mix the almonds, lemon-rind and cinnamon together, and put ½ into the pie-dish. Cover with thin slices of roll, then add the rest of the almond mixture, and again cover with slices of roll. Boil the milk, and add to it the sugar; beat the eggs well, then pour on to them the hot, NOT BOILING, milk, and stir well. Now add the milk, etc. to the rest of the ingredients in the pie-dish, but in table-spoonfuls to avoid floating the slices of roll. Cover the pudding and let it stand for ½ an hour, then bake it gently for about an hour. Serve either hot or cold.

APPLE AMBER PUDDING.

With 6 large apples take 3 oz. of brown sugar, 2 oz. of butter, 3 eggs, 1 lemon, cherries, strips of angelica, some short-paste, or puff-paste trimmings, and castor sugar. Sufficient for 6 or 7 persons.

Line the edge of a pie-dish with thin strips of paste about 3 inches wide, and decorate the edge with overlapping leaves or small rounds of pastry, which must be securely fixed by means of white of egg. Peel and slice the apples, stew them gently with the butter, sugar, and lemon-rind, until tender, then pass through a fine sieve, and add the yolks of eggs. Pour the mixture into the pie-dish, bake gently for 20 minutes, then pile the stiffly-whisked whites of eggs on the top. Dredge liberally with castor sugar, decorate with cherries and angelica, and replace in the oven until the whites of eggs harden and acquire a little colour. Serve either hot or cold.

APPLE PUDDING, BAKED.

To 6 sour cooking apples allow ½ a pint of breadcrumbs, 2 or 3 tablespoonfuls of sugar, 1 oz. of butter and 1 egg. Sufficient for 3 or 4 persons.

Pare, core and cut the apples into slices, put them into a stewpan with the sugar and 2 or 3 tablespoonfuls of water, cook until tender, then stir in the butter and well-beaten egg. Coat the bottom and sides of a well-buttered pie-dish thickly with breadcrumbs, add the apple pulp, cover with the remainder of the breadcrumbs, put a few pieces of butter on the top, and bake gently for about ¾ of an hour, keeping the dish covered with greased paper to prevent the surface from becoming too brown. Serve either hot or cold.

APRICOT PUDDING, BAKED.

Take 1 tin or bottle of apricots, ¾ of a pint of fresh bread-crumbs, 3 tablespoonfuls of moist sugar, 1 pint of milk, 2 eggs, the juice of 1 lemon, a glass of sherry (optional), and some Short-crust paste (p. 87). Sufficient for 6 or 7 persons.

Boil the milk, pour it on the breadcrumbs, and let them soak for ½ an hour. Rub the apricots through a hair sieve, add to them the lemon-juice, sugar, sherry (if used), 2 yolks of egg, and mix well together. Have ready a pie-dish with the edges lined, as directed for **Apple Amber** (p. 89), add the milk and breadcrumbs to the rest of the ingredients, pour into the pie-dish, and bake in a steady oven until set. Whisk the whites to a stiff froth, add to them 1 tablespoonful of castor sugar, and when the pastry is three parts baked, and the apricot mixture set, pile them on the top of the pudding. The surface should be liberally sprinkled with castor sugar ; and it may also be decorated with strips of crystallized apricots. Return to the oven, and bake until the méringue acquires a pale fawn colour. Serve either hot or cold.

CABINET PUDDING, COLD.

Procure some Savoy biscuits, 2 oz. of ratafias, ½ a pint of milk, ½ a gill of cream, 1 oz. of castor sugar, ½ an oz. of leaf gelatine, 3 eggs, glacé cherries, vanilla essence, and some Wine jelly (p. 60). Sufficient for 1 medium-sized mould.

Decorate the bottom of a charlotte-mould, previously lined with a layer of jelly, with halves or rings of cherries, and line the sides of the mould with biscuits, placing them alternately back and front next the tin. Bring the milk nearly to boiling-point, add the eggs previously beaten up, and stir by the side of the fire until they thicken. Dissolve the gelatine and sugar in 1 or 2 tablespoonfuls of water, strain into the custard, and add vanilla essence to taste. Place the ratafias and trimmings of the Savoy biscuits in the mould, add the cream to the custard when cool, and pour into the mould. Let it stand in a cool place until set, then turn out and serve.

CARAMEL PUDDING.

For the caramel : take 2 oz. of loaf sugar and 2 tablespoonfuls of cold water. For the custard : ½ a pint of milk, 2 eggs, 1 tablespoonful of castor sugar, and a few drops of vanilla or other flavouring. Sufficient for 4 or 5 persons.

Boil the loaf sugar and cold water together until the liquid acquires a light-brown colour, then pour it into a charlotte or plain timbale-mould, and turn the mould slowly round and round until every part of it is coated with the caramel. Beat the eggs, add to them the sugar, flavouring and milk, and stir until the sugar is dissolved. Strain the custard into the mould, cover with a greased paper, steam very slowly for about 40 minutes, then turn out carefully. No other sauce is needed than the caramel, which runs off when the pudding is inverted. This pudding is equally nice served hot or cold ; when intended to be served cold it may be allowed to cool before being turned out of the mould, and so lessen the probability of its breaking. If preferred, 6 dariole-moulds may be used instead of 1 large mould.

CARAMEL RICE PUDDING.

For the caramel : take 4 oz. of loaf sugar and ¼ of a pint of water. For the pudding : 3 oz. of rice, 1 pint of milk, 1 tablespoonful of castor sugar, 2 eggs and vanilla essence. Sufficient for 5 or 6 persons.

Prepare the caramel, and line the mould as directed in the preceding recipe. Simmer the rice in the milk until tender, cool slightly, then stir in the well-beaten eggs, sugar, and a few drops of vanilla essence. Turn into the prepared mould, cover with buttered paper, and steam for nearly 1 hour. Serve either hot or cold. If preferred, the rice may be steamed in dariole-moulds.

DANISH PUDDING.

With 1 breakfastcupful of tapioca take 1 breakfastcupful of red-currant jelly, salt, castor sugar, and 3 pints of water.

Soak the tapioca in the water for at least 12 hours, then turn it into a double saucepan, cook for about 1½ hours, and add salt and sugar to taste. Stir in the jelly, and, when well mixed, turn the preparation into a mould, and put aside until set. Serve with whipped cream.

FRUIT PUDDING.

Take 1 lb. of fruit stewed, and 6 stale sponge cakes.

Cut the sponge cake into ½-inch slices, and with them line a pudding basin. Stew the fruit in a jar until tender, sweeten to taste, and pour both fruit and syrup into the basin. Cover with slices of cake, press it down with a plate and weight until cold. Serve with Custard sauce (p. 30). For a plain pudding, stale bread may be used instead of cake.

ITALIAN PUDDING.

To 1 lb. of apples sliced allow ½ a lb. of dates stoned, ½ a lb. of raisins stoned, 2 oz. of mixed peel shredded, 2 oz. of Savoy or other plain cake-crumbs, 2 eggs, ¾ of a pint of milk, sugar, and a little nutmeg. Sufficient for 5 or 6 persons.

Make a custard of the eggs and milk, stir in the cake-crumbs, and sweeten to taste. Mix the dates, raisins, and peel together, and add a little nutmeg. Place the apple at the bottom of a pie-dish, add the mixed fruit, and pour in the custard. Bake in a rather cool oven for ¾ of an hour, and serve either hot or cold.

JENNY LIND PUDDING.

Have ready 4 stale sponge cakes, 4 coco-nut cakes, 12 rata-fias, 2 eggs, 1 pint of milk, sugar, and 1 tablespoonful of desiccated coco-nut. Sufficient for 5 or 6 persons.

Slice the sponge cakes, and place them in a buttered pie-dish interspersed with the coco-nut cakes and ratafias. Simmer the coco-nut in the milk for about 20 minutes, cool slightly, add the eggs and sugar to taste, and stir by the side of the fire for a few minutes. Pour the custard into the pie-dish, bake gently until set, then serve either hot or cold.

LEMON PUDDING, BAKED.

Take 2 lemons, 2 oz. of castor sugar, 1 oz. of butter, 3 sponge cakes, 1 egg, ½ a pint of milk and some paste.

Put the milk, butter, sugar and grated lemon-rind into a stewpan, boil up, let it infuse for about 15 minutes, then pour over the well-beaten yolk of egg, stirring meanwhile. Add the crumbled sponge cakes and lemon-juice, mix well together, and pour into a pie-dish, the edges of which must be previously lined and decorated with the paste (*see* **Apple Amber,** p. 89). Bake in a moderate oven from 30 to 35 minutes, or until the mixture is set, then cover with the stiffly-whisked white of egg, and dredge liberally with castor sugar. Replace in the oven until the méringue hardens and acquires a little colour. Serve either hot or cold.

ORANGE PUDDING.

Procure 4 oranges, 3 oz. of castor sugar, 3 oz. of cake-crumbs or crumbled sponge cakes, 2 eggs, ½ a pint of milk, salt, nutmeg and Short-crust paste (p. 87). Sufficient for 5 or 6 persons.

Remove the rind of 1 orange in exceedingly thin strips, place them in a stewpan with the milk, and bring to boiling-point. Let the preparation infuse for about 20 minutes, then pour it over the cake-crumbs, add the sugar, a pinch of salt, a sprinkling of nutmeg, the well-beaten eggs, and the juice of the oranges. Have ready a pie-dish with the edges lined as directed for **Apple Amber** (p. 89), pour in the preparation, and bake in a moderate oven for about ½ an hour. Dredge with castor sugar, and serve either hot or cold.

ORLEANS PUDDING.

Have ready some lemon or wine jelly, crystallized fruit, kirsch, ½ a pint of milk, 4 oz. of vanilla sugar, 3 eggs, ½ a pint of whipped cream, 2 oz. of gelatine, Genoese or sponge cake.

Take a plain pudding mould, and in the bottom place a
little jelly flavoured with kirsch, and decorate same, when
set, with a few neatly cut crystallized fruits. Mix together
a Bavaroise cream consisting of ½ a pint of milk, 4 oz. of
sugar (vanilla), and 3 yolks of eggs. Mix the same as for
vanilla ice, then let it stand until cold ; next add ½ a pint of
whipped cream, and stir in 2 oz. of dissolved gelatine. Half
fill the mould with this and mix in some small pieces of sand-
wiched Genoese Cake, flavoured with kirsch or maraschino.
Fill up the mould with the remainder of the Bavaroise
cream and let stand until set. When ready to be served
turn it out carefully on to a silver dish, and pour round the
cream a raspberry sauce.

PORCUPINE PUDDING.

With 1¼ pints of milk take 6 stale sponge cakes, 2 oz. of
loaf sugar, 3 eggs, 1 oz. of almonds, raspberry jam, and vanilla
pod. Sufficient for 5 or 6 persons.

Put 1 pint of milk, the flavouring ingredient, and the sugar
into a jug, add the eggs well beaten, and place the jug in a
saucepan of boiling water. Stir the contents until thick
enough to coat the spoon, then transfer the jug to a basin
of cold water, and stir frequently until the custard is cold.
Meanwhile, blanch the almonds and shred them lengthwise.
Split each sponge cake in two, spread on a thick layer of jam,
replace the halves, and arrange them compactly in a glass
dish. Prick them well with a fork, pour the remainder of
the milk slowly over them, and stick in the almonds. Let
them soak for a few minutes, then pour over the custard and
serve.

POUDING À LA DIPLOMATE (ICED).

Take 2 oz. sultanas, 1 oz. currants, 2 oz. glacé cherries,
2 apricots, finger biscuits and Maraschino ; for the custard,
1 pint milk, 3 eggs, ½ a gill of cream, and vanilla flavouring :
½ oz. gelatine, olive oil, glacé cherries and angelica.

Put into a basin the sultanas and currants, and pour over
enough hot water to cover ; let it stand for 10 minutes, then
drain off the water and add 2 oz. of glacé cherries, cut in
quarters, also 2 apricots cut into slices, flavour with Maraschino and cover.

Prepare a custard with the milk, eggs, vanilla flavouring

COLD SWEETS

1. Savoy or Sponge Mould.   2. Ratafia Trifle.

COLD SWEETS

1. Fancy Genoese Pastry.   2. Gooseberry Tart.   3. Cherry Tartlets.

and cream. When the egg liaison is formed, strain the custard and add the dissolved gelatine. Brush over lightly the inside of a timbale or charlotte mould with olive oil and decorate with slices of glacé cherries and angelica. Cover this with a layer of prepared cream. On this put a layer of finger biscuits, crushed up and moistened in the Maraschino syrup; upon this put a layer of prepared fruit and cover again with a layer of custard. Continue this until the mould is filled. Place it on a bed of crushed ice to set. Unmould when required for table.

QUEEN MAB'S PUDDING.

To 1 pint of milk allow 3 oz. of castor sugar, 1 oz. of gelatine, ¼ of a pint of double cream, 3 eggs, 2 oz. of glacé cherries halved, 1 oz. of candied citron peel shredded, and vanilla essence. Sufficient for 5 or 6 persons.

Soak the gelatine in the milk for ½ an hour, then stir it over the fire until dissolved, and add the sugar. Cool slightly, put in the yolks of eggs and cream, stir by the fire until the mixture thickens, but it must not boil. Let it cool, add the cherries, citron, and vanilla to taste, stir until on the point of setting, then turn into a mould previously lined with jelly, or rinsed with cold water.

ST. CLOUD PUDDING.

Make 1 pint of strong clear coffee (coffee essence may be used), and take 3 eggs, 2 oz. of almonds, 2 oz. of castor sugar, stale sponge cake (or any plain cake), 3 tablespoonfuls of apricot marmalade or jam, ½ a gill of cream, butter, glacé cherries, and angelica. Sufficient for 6 or 7 persons.

Blanch, shred, and bake the almonds pale brown. Coat a plain charlotte-mould thickly with clarified butter, and sprinkle liberally with the prepared almonds when cold. Three-quarters fill the mould with pieces of cake, interspersing the remainder of the almonds. Dissolve the sugar in the coffee, pour over the well-beaten eggs, stirring meanwhile, and add the cream. Strain into the mould, cover with a buttered paper, and steam very gently for about 2 hours. Turn out and set aside till cold. Dilute the apricot marmalade with a little water, sweeten to taste, and when cool strain over the pudding. Decorate with rings of cherries and strips of angelica.

C.S.   F

SAXON PUDDING.

Procure 4 sponge cakes, 6 macaroons, 18 ratafias, 2 eggs, ½ a pint of milk, ¼ of a pint of cream, 1 glass of sherry (optional), 2 oz. of almonds, a few glacé cherries, angelica and vanilla essence. Sufficient for 5 or 6 persons.

Blanch, peel, shred and bake the almonds until nicely browned. Butter a plain charlotte-mould, decorate the bottom with halves of cherries and strips of angelica, and sprinkle the sides thickly with the prepared almonds. Fill the mould with alternate layers of slices of sponge cake, pieces of macaroon and ratafias. Beat the eggs well, add the milk, cream, wine (if used), and a few drops of vanilla. Pour this into the mould, cover with a buttered paper, and let the mixture stand for 1 hour. Then steam from 1½ to 1¾ hours, and serve with fruit syrup, or other suitable sauce. This pudding is exceedingly nice cold, with whipped cream as an accompaniment.

SOMERSETSHIRE PUDDING.

Have ready 3 eggs, their weight in flour, and the weight of 2 eggs in castor sugar and butter, and essence of vanilla, or other flavouring. Sufficient for 6 or 7 persons.

Cream the butter and sugar together until thick and smooth, and add each egg separately. Beat well, then stir in the flour and add milk gradually until the mixture drops readily from the spoon. Turn the preparation into well-buttered darioles or cups, bake gently for 20 minutes, or until done. When cold, scoop the insides out and fill the cavities with jam or stewed fruit and cream.

TIPSY PUDDING.

Take 4 oz. of flour, 3 oz. of castor sugar, 2 eggs, 3 or 4 tablespoonfuls of rum, and desiccated coco-nut. Sufficient for 6 or 7 persons.

Beat the eggs and sugar together until thick and smooth, and stir in the flour as lightly as possible. Coat 6 or 7 well-buttered dariole-moulds thickly with castor sugar, fill them ¾ full with the mixture, and bake in a moderately hot oven. When cooked, baste them with rum sweetened to taste, and sprinkle lightly with coco-nut.

CHAPTER VI

PASTRY FOR COLD SWEETS

THE quality especially to be desired in pastry is lightness, and this depends almost entirely upon the amount of cold air contained in the pastry when expansion takes place in the oven.

The best pastry is, therefore, that which contains the greatest quantity of the coldest air prior to baking. The repeated foldings and rollings to which puff-paste is subjected have this increase of air in view. The difference between puff, or flaky and short-crust pastry is that in the former there are thin layers of air and pastry alternating, and in the latter the air fills small cavities all over the paste.

BAKING

All kinds of pastry should be baked in a moderately hot oven. A high temperature is necessary to expand the air or gas, and thus make the pastry light, and also to burst the grains in the flour, thereby enabling these to absorb the fat immediately it melts.

Unless the heat is sufficiently great to act upon the flour in this manner, the melted fat runs out and leaves the pastry less rich, and also, probably, both heavy and tough.

An oven with a good bottom heat is desirable for baking tarts and tartlets; when heated from above it is advisable to bake, or partially bake, the tarts before filling them.

PASTRY (to Keep).

Pastry not intended for immediate use should be carefully wrapped in grease-proof or buttered paper, and kept in a cool place.

RECIPES FOR PASTRY, CRUST, ETC.

BUTTER CRUST. (For Boiled Puddings.)

With 1 lb. of flour take 6 oz. of butter and ½ a pint of water. Sufficient for 1½ lb. of pastry.

With a knife mix the flour to a smooth paste, adding the water gradually. Roll out thinly, place the butter over it in small pieces, dredge lightly with flour, and fold the paste over. Roll out again, and use as required.

CHOUX PASTRY.

Have ready 4 oz. of fine flour, 4 oz. of butter, 2 oz. of sugar, 2 eggs, ½ a pint of water, salt, and vanilla-essence or other flavouring.

Put the water, butter, sugar, and a good pinch of salt into a stewpan, and when boiling add the flour, previously well dried and sieved, and stir and cook gently for at least 10 minutes. Let it cool a little, then beat in the eggs one at a time, add a few drops of the flavouring ingredient, and use as required.

FLAKY PASTRY. (For Pies, Tarts and Tartlets.)

To 12 oz. of fine, dry, sieved flour allow 9 oz. of fresh butter (or butter and lard mixed may be used if the strictest economy is absolutely essential), and about ¼ of a pint of water.

Sieve the flour into a basin, and rub in lightly a third of the butter. Add the water and mix into a smooth paste, more or less moist, according to the consistency of the butter, with which it must agree in this respect; roll it out into a long, narrow strip. Divide the remainder of the butter into three equal portions; put one portion on the paste in small pieces, dredge lightly with flour, fold it evenly in three, turn it round so as to have the folded edges to the right and left when rolling, press the edges lightly with the rolling-pin, to prevent the air escaping, and roll out as before. Repeat this process with the other portions of butter. The pastry may be used at once, but it will be lighter if allowed to stand for 1 hour in a cool place before being used. In making up, handle as lightly and roll as evenly as possible. Bake in a hot oven, and avoid opening the oven door until the pastry has risen and become partially baked.

GENOESE PASTE.

Take 3 oz. of fine flour, 4 oz. of castor sugar, 2 oz. of butter and 3 eggs. Sufficient for a medium-sized cake.

Dry and sieve the flour, separate the whites of the eggs from the yolks, to the latter add the sugar, work vigorously until it has a thick creamy appearance, then stir in the butter melted. Whisk the whites to a stiff froth, stir in the flour, then mix lightly, but thoroughly, with the contents of the other basin. Pour the mixture into a papered buttered tin, and bake in a moderately hot oven.

GENOESE PASTRY. (Another Method.)

Have ready 3 oz. of fine flour, 3 oz. of butter, 4 oz. of castor sugar, and 3 eggs. Sufficient for a medium-sized cake.

Break the eggs into a basin, add the sugar, place the basin over a saucepan of boiling water and whisk until lukewarm. Now remove the basin and continue the whisking until the mixture becomes thick and creamy, then add the butter melted, and stir in the previously-sifted flour as lightly as possible. Have ready a well-buttered papered tin, pour in the mixture, and bake for about ½ an hour in a moderately hot oven.

HALF-PUFF-PASTE. (*See* recipe on p. 86 for **Puff-Paste, Rough.**)

PÂTE BRISÉE OR FRENCH CRUST.

Procure 1 lb. of fine, dry and sieved flour, 6 oz. of fresh butter, 2 eggs, ½ a saltspoonful of salt and about ½ a pint of cold water.

Sieve the flour, add the salt, rub the butter lightly in, and mix into a smooth paste with the eggs and water, adding the latter gradually as the paste must be very firm.

PUFF-PASTE. (For Pies, Tarts and Tartlets, Bouchées, etc.)

With 1 lb. of flour, take 1 lb. of butter, 1 teaspoonful of lemon-juice, and about ⅓ of a pint of cold water.

Wash and squeeze the butter in cold water, dry well in a floured cloth, shape into a square about the size of a slice of sandwich bread, and keep in a cool place while the paste is being prepared. Sieve the flour on to a marble slab, or board, make a well in the centre, put in the lemon-juice, and add water gradually until a smooth paste is formed. The condition of the butter determines the consistency; when soft, the paste must be equally so. Knead the paste until smooth, then roll it out into a strip a little wider than the butter, and rather more than twice its length. Place the butter on one half of the paste, fold the other half over, enclosing the butter entirely, and press the edges together with the rolling pin. Let it remain in a cool place for about 15 minutes, then roll out to about three times the original length, but keeping the width the same, and fold exactly in three. Turn the paste round so that the folded edges are on the right and left, roll and fold again, and put aside for 15 minutes. Repeat this until the paste has been rolled out six times. The rolling should be done as evenly as possible, and the paste kept in a long narrow shape which, when folded, forms a square. Each time the paste is rolled out it may be well sprinkled with flour, but it must be evenly distributed with a paste-brush, and all the loose flour carefully brushed off before beginning to roll. When the paste has had its sixth roll it is ready for use; it should be baked in a hot oven, and until the paste has risen and become partially baked, the oven door should not be opened, because a current of cold air may cause the flakes to collapse on one side.

PUFF-PASTE, ROUGH, OR HALF-PUFF-PASTE.
(For Pies, Tarts and Tartlets.)

To 8 oz. of flour allow 6 oz. of butter (or equal quantities of butter and lard), $\frac{1}{2}$ a teaspoonful of lemon-juice, salt, and about $\frac{1}{4}$ of a pint of water. Sufficient for an average-sized pie.

Sieve the flour on to a pasteboard, divide the butter into pieces about the size of a small walnut and mix them lightly with the flour. Make a well in the centre, put in the lemon-juice, salt, and 1 tablespoonful of water, mix lightly, keeping the pieces of butter intact, and add water gradually, until a moderately stiff paste is formed. Roll into a long strip, fold it equally in three, turn it round so as to have the folded edges to the right and left, and roll out as before. Repeat until the paste has been rolled out four times, then use; or, if convenient, let it remain for 1 hour in a cool place before being used.

RICH SHORT-CRUST. (For Pies, Tarts, etc.)

Take 1 lb. of flour, ¾ of a lb. of butter, 2 yolks of eggs, 1 level tablespoonful of castor sugar, and 1 teaspoonful of baking-powder. Sufficient for 2 medium-sized tarts.

Rub the butter lightly into the flour, add the baking-powder, sugar, yolks of eggs, and a little water if necessary, but this paste must be rather stiff, and when the butter is soft, or the paste is being mixed in a warm place, only a few drops of water may be required. Roll out thinly and use at once. The crust for fruit tarts should be lightly brushed over with cold water, and dredged with castor sugar before being baked.

SHORT-CRUST. (For Pies, Tarts, etc.)

Procure 8 oz. of flour, 2 oz. of butter, 2 oz. of lard, 1 yolk of egg, 1 teaspoonful of baking-powder, a good pinch of salt, and about ⅛ of a pint of water. Sufficient for 1 medium-sized tart.

Rub the butter and lard lightly into the flour, add the baking-powder, salt, yolk of egg, and sufficient water to form a stiff paste. Roll out to the required thickness and use at once.

SHORT-CRUST, PLAIN. (For Pies, Tarts, etc.)

Have ready ½ a lb. of flour, 3 oz. of lard, clarified fat or dripping, 1 teaspoonful of baking-powder (heaped), ¼ of a teaspoonful of salt, and about ¼ of a pint of water. Sufficient for 1 medium-sized tart.

Pass the flour, salt and baking-powder through a sieve into a large basin, then rub in the fat, add the water, and work into a smooth dough with a knife. Roll out to desired shape and thickness, and use at once. When required for fruit tarts, 1 tablespoonful of sugar should be added to the above ingredients.

SUET CRUST.

With 12 oz. of flour, take 4 oz. of suet, 1 teaspoonful of baking-powder, ¼ of a teaspoonful of salt, and about ⅛ of a pint of water. Sufficient for 1 large pudding.

Chop the suet finely with a little of the flour, mix it with the other dry ingredients, and add water to form a moderately stiff dough. Roll out and use at once.

SUET CRUST, RICH. (For Puddings, etc.)

To 8 oz. of flour, allow 3 oz. of breadcrumbs, 6 oz. of suet, 1 heaped teaspoonful of baking-powder, $\frac{1}{4}$ of a teaspoonful of salt and about $\frac{1}{3}$ of a pint of water.   Sufficient for 1 fair-sized pudding.

Free the suet from skin, shed and chop it finely.   Mix well together the flour, breadcrumbs, suet, salt and baking-powder, and add water to form a dough soft enough to roll out easily, but not sufficiently moist to stick to the board and rolling-pin. This pastry makes an exceedingly light and easily-digested pudding, but in consequence of its extreme lightness it is liable to break if turned out of the basin.

SWEET PASTRY. (For Tartlets.)

Procure 1 lb. of fine flour, 8 oz. of castor sugar, 5 oz. of butter, 1 egg, and the finely-grated rind of $\frac{1}{2}$ a lemon.

Sieve the flour into a basin, make a well in the centre, put in the sugar, lemon rind, butter and egg, and mix the whole into a stiff dough.   Roll out and use as required.

TO GLAZE PASTRY.

Fruit tarts, puffs, etc., are usually brushed lightly over with cold water, and sprinkled liberally with castor sugar before baking.   Or, when a thin coating of icing is desired, they are, when nearly baked, brushed over with well-beaten white of egg, and well-dredged with castor sugar.

CHAPTER VII

RECIPES FOR CHEESECAKES, TARTS, TARTLETS, ETC.

ALMOND CHEESECAKES.

Make sufficient short-crust paste (p. 87) to line 9 or 10 patty-pans, and take 4 oz. of ground almonds, 4 oz. of castor sugar, ¾ of an oz. of cornflour, ½ an oz. of butter, 1 egg, raspberry or strawberry jam, and nutmeg.

Beat the egg, add it gradually to the cornflour, and stir until perfectly smooth. Add the sugar, almonds, butter melted, and a pinch of nutmeg. Line 9 or 10 patty-pans with short-crust paste, spread about ½ a teaspoonful of jam on the bottom of each one, and fill with the mixture. Bake from 20 to 25 minutes in a moderately hot oven.

APPLE AMBER.

With 6 large apples, take 3 oz. of moist sugar, 2 oz. of butter, 2 eggs, ½ a lemon, paste trimmings, or 4 oz. of short-crust paste (p. 87), ground cinnamon, and ground cloves. Sufficient for 6 or 7 persons.

Peel, core and slice the apples, put them into the stewpan with sugar, and 1 tablespoonful of water, simmer gently until tender, then rub through a hair sieve. Return the apple pulp to the stewpan, add the lemon-rind finely grated, lemon-juice, and a good pinch each of cloves and cinnamon. Re-heat, then stir in the butter and yolks of eggs, and cook until the mixture thickens. Meanwhile line the edges of the dish with paste, and ornament the extreme edge with small leaves or rounds of the same, arranged slightly to overlap each other. Pour in the apple preparation, and bake in a moderate oven until set. Have ready the whites of eggs whisked to a stiff froth, and sweetened with a little castor sugar, arrange in a rocky form on the top of the pudding, sprinkle liberally with

castor sugar, and, if liked, decorate with cherries or candied
fruits. Replace in the oven until the méringue hardens and
acquires a little colour, and serve either hot or cold.

APPLE CHEESECAKES.

To 1½ lb. of apples, allow 3 oz. of sugar, 1 oz. of butter, 2
eggs, 1 lemon, and short-crust paste (p. 87).

Peel, core and slice the apples, place them in a stewpan
with the sugar, and 1 tablespoonful of water, simmer gently
until tender, and rub them through a hair sieve. Return the
pulp to the stewpan, add the butter, lemon-juice and rind
finely grated, re-heat, stir in the yolks of 2 eggs and the white
of one, and cook until the mixture thickens. Have ready the
patty-pans lined with paste and partially baked, fill with the
apple preparation, cover lightly with stiffly-whisked sweetened
white of egg, and bake in a moderate oven for 15 minutes.

APPLE TART.

Have ready 2 lb. of apples, 2 tablepoonfuls of moist sugar,
4 cloves, or a ¼ of a teaspoonful of grated lemon-rind, and
short-crust paste (p. 87). Sufficient for 6 or 7 persons.

Peel, core and cut the apples into thick slices. Roll the
paste into an oval form a little larger than the top of the pie-
dish, invert the dish in the centre of the paste, and cut round,
leaving a ¼-inch margin on all sides. Line the edge of the pie-
dish with the trimmings, put in half the apples, add the sugar
and flavouring ingredient, then the remainder of the fruit.
Moisten the paste lining the edge of the dish with water, put
on the cover, press the edges together, and notch them at
intervals of about ⅛ of an inch. Bake in a brisk oven from
40 to 50 minutes, and when the paste has risen and set, brush
it over lightly with cold water, and dredge well with castor
sugar. This must be done quickly, and the tart immediately
replaced in the oven. If the tart is to be eaten cold, directly
it leaves the oven the crust should be raised gently with a
knife, to allow some of the steam to escape, otherwise it may
lose some of its crispness.

APRICOT BOUCHÉES.

Prepare some puff-paste (p. 85), and take 1 tin of preserved apricots, castor sugar, and ¼ of a pint of stiffly-whipped
cream. Sufficient for 6 or more persons.

When the paste has had the necessary number of turns, roll it out to rather less than ½ an inch in thickness. With a hot wet cutter stamp out some rounds about 2 inches in diameter, and make a deep, circular indentation with a smaller cutter. Bake in a quick oven for about 12 minutes, and when cool scoop out the paste within the ring. Meanwhile well drain the apricots from the syrup, put ½ an apricot, the rounded side down, into each case, and fill the hollow with stiffly-whipped sweetened cream.

APRICOT TART.

With 1 tin of apricots, allow sugar to taste, and short-crust paste (p. 87). Sufficient for 6 or 7 persons.

Place the apricots in a pie-dish, sprinkle with sugar, and half fill the dish with the syrup from the tin. Cover with paste (*see* **Apple Tart,** p. 90), and bake in a quick oven from 30 to 40 minutes. When the paste has risen and set, brush it over lightly with cold water, and dredge well with castor sugar. Return quickly to the oven, and finish baking.

BAKEWELL TART.

Make ½ a lb. of short-crust paste (p. 87), and have ready some raspberry jam, 2 oz. of ground almonds, 2 oz. of castor sugar, 2 oz. of butter, 1 egg, and essence of almonds. Sufficient for 7 or 8 persons.

Cream the butter and sugar together until thick and white, stir in the egg, add the almonds, also a few drops of essence of almonds, and beat well. Line a flat dish with the pastry, place a good layer of jam on the bottom, and spread the mixture lightly on the top of it. Bake in a quick oven for about ½ an hour, and serve either hot or cold, according to taste.

BALMORAL TARTLETS.

Take 1 oz. of butter, 1 oz. of castor sugar, ½ an oz. of cake-crumbs, ½ an oz. of glacé cherries cut into small dice, ½ an oz. of candied peel finely shredded, ¾ of an oz. of cornflour, or potato flour, 1 egg, and short-crust paste (p. 87). Sufficient for 12 small tartlets.

Make the paste as directed, and line 12 patty-pans. Cream the butter and sugar until thick and white, stir in the yolk of the egg, add the cake-crumbs, cherries, peel and cornflour.

Whisk the white of egg stiffly, stir it in lightly, and fill the patty-cases with the preparation. Cross two narrow strips of paste on the top of each tartlet, and bake for about 20 minutes in a moderate oven.

BLACK-CURRANT TARTLETS.

Prepare sufficient short-crust (p. 87), to line 12 patty-pans, and procure 1 lb. of black-currants, 2 tablespoonfuls of moist sugar, ¼ of a pint of cream (if liked), and castor sugar.

Cook the black-currants with the sugar, and 2 tablespoonfuls of water, in a jar, on the stove or in a slow oven. Line 12 patty-pans with the paste, fill them with rice placed in buttered papers, and bake until crisp in a brisk oven. When cold, fill them with the prepared cold fruit and syrup, cover with stiffly-whipped, sweetened cream (if used), and serve cold.

CHERRY TARTLETS.

With ½ a lb. of short-crust paste (p. 87), take 1 lb. of cooking cherries, 2 tablespoonfuls of moist sugar, 2 eggs, and castor sugar. Sufficient for about 12 tartlets.

Remove the stalks from the cherries, put them into a small stewjar with the moist sugar, stand the jar in a saucepan, surround it with boiling water, and cook until the cherries are tender. Meanwhile line 10 or 12 deep patty-pans with the paste, fill them with rice in order to prevent blistering (rice should be kept for this purpose and used over and over again), placing a buttered paper between it and the paste, and bake in a quick oven. When the cherries are sufficiently cooked, strain off the syrup into a small stewpan, add the yolks of eggs previously beaten, and stir by the side of the fire until the custard thickens. Fill the patty-cases with cherries, cover with a layer of custard, on the top spread a little stiffly-whisked white of egg, and sprinkle with castor sugar. Replace in the oven until the white of egg hardens, and acquires a little colour, then serve hot or cold.

CHESTNUT AMBER.

Have ready ½ a pint of chestnuts, ½ a pint of milk, 2 oz. of breadcrumbs, 1 oz. of castor sugar, 1 oz. of butter, 2 eggs, 1 lemon, vanilla essence, and puff-paste (p. 85). Sufficient for 5 or 6 persons.

Bake or roast the chestnuts for about 20 minutes, and remove
the skins. Put them into a stewpan, with just sufficient
water to cover the bottom of the pan, simmer gently until
tender, and rub through a fine sieve. Simmer the thinly-cut
rind of the lemon and the milk for 15 or 20 minutes, and
strain it over the breadcrumbs. Cream the butter and sugar
together until thick and smooth, add the yolks of the eggs,
the juice of the lemon, a few drops of vanilla essence, and stir
in the chestnuts, breadcrumbs and milk. Have the pie-dish
ready lined with paste, as directed for **Apple Amber,** pour
in the mixture, and bake in a moderately hot oven from 25
to 30 minutes, or until the mixture is firm and brown, and the
paste sufficiently cooked. Whisk the whites to a stiff froth,
sweeten with a little sugar, pile lightly on the top of the pudding, and dredge well with castor sugar. Return to the oven
until the méringue is set and acquires a little colour.

CHOCOLATE TARTLETS.

Make sufficient short-crust paste (p. 87), to line 12 patty
pans, and take 2 oz. of grated chocolate, 4 oz. of cake-crumbs, 3
oz. of castor sugar, 2 oz. of butter, ½ an oz. of cornflour, 2 eggs,
and chocolate icing (p. 101).

Cream the yolks of the eggs and sugar well together, add
the cake-crumbs, chocolate, cornflour, and the butter melted.
Whisk the whites of eggs stiffly, and stir them in as lightly as
possible. Have ready 12 patty-pans lined with short-paste,
fill them with the mixture, and bake in a moderately hot oven
from 20 to 25 minutes. When cold, cover the surface of each
tartlet with chocolate icing, allow it to harden, then serve.

COFFEE ÉCLAIRS.

To ½ a pint of milk, allow 2 oz. of butter, 2 oz. of cornflour,
2 oz. of Vienna flour, 2 eggs, ½ a teaspoonful of vanilla essence,
a pinch of salt, 1 oz. of castor sugar, Moka custard for filling,
and coffee icing (p. 101). Sufficient for 10 or 12 éclairs.

Put the water, butter, sugar and salt into a stewpan, when
boiling, stir in the cornflour and Vienna flour (previously
mixed), work it with a wooden spoon over the fire sufficiently
long to produce a soft paste which will leave the side and
bottom of the pan clean. Draw the stewpan from the fire,
add the flavouring essence, and work the eggs in gradually
(leaving out 1 white). Beat the paste well for some minutes,

then put it in a large forcing or savoy bag with a plain tube, and force out even-sized shapes, similar to finger biscuits, on to a lightly-buttered baking-tin, about 1 inch apart from each other. Bake to a nice fawn colour in a moderate oven. When done, split the sides with a sharp knife, and fill each with 1 teaspoonful of Moka custard. Have ready some coffee icing, and dip each éclair into it, so as to cover the surface and sides well and smoothly. Place the éclairs on a wire tray to set, and dish up when required.

CREAM TARTLETS.

Make some short-crust paste (p. 87), and have ready apricot jam, ⅛ of a pint of cream, and castor sugar.

Line 10 or 12 patty-pans with the paste, fill them with rice, with buttered paper between it and the paste, and bake until crisp in a brisk oven (about 10 minutes). When cool, remove the rice and then about half fill them with jam, pile the stiffly-whipped sweetened cream on the top, and serve cold.

CUSTARD TARTLETS.

Prepare sufficient short-crust paste (p. 87), to line 12 deep patty-pans, and take 2 whole eggs, 2 whites of eggs, 1 pint of milk, and sugar.

Line 12 deep patty-tins with short-paste. Beat the 2 eggs, add the milk, and sweeten to taste. Fill the patty-pans with custard and bake in a moderate oven until set (from 25 to 30 minutes). Have ready the whites of eggs stiffly whisked and sweetened, pile lightly on the tartlets, and replace them in the oven until the méringue hardens, and acquires a little colour. Serve cold.

ÉCLAIRS.

Take some choux paste (p. 84), chocolate or coffee icing (p. 101), cream, and confectioners' custard (p. 102), or jam.

Put the choux paste into a forcing-bag, and press it out on to a buttered baking-sheet in the form of small savoy biscuits. Or, if a bag and pipe are not available, roll it on a floured board to the same shape. Bake from 15 to 20 minutes in a moderate oven, let them cool on a sieve, then make an incision on the side of them and scoop out the soft interior. Fill the cavities with stiffly-whipped sweetened cream, confectioners' custard or jam, and coat them with chocolate or coffee icing.

FLAN OF APPLES.

With 3 or 4 apples, take 1 tablespoonful of moist sugar, 2 tablespoonfuls of sherry (optional), 4 cloves, 2 whites of eggs, castor sugar, and ½ a lb. of short-crust paste (p. 87). Sufficient for 4 or 5 persons.

Peel, core and cut each apple into 8 sections, place them in a stewpan, add the cloves and sherry (if used), cover closely, stand the stewpan in a tin containing boiling water, and cook until tender, but not sufficiently so as to break easily. Meanwhile line a 6-inch diameter flan or paste-ring with paste rolled out to about ¼-inch in thickness, fill it with rice placed on an interlining of buttered paper, and bake in a quick oven. When done, remove the rice and paper, fill with the apples, arranged in a pyramid, strain the juice (if any) over them, and sprinkle well with sugar. Whisk the whites of eggs to a stiff froth, spread it lightly over the apples, dredge well with castor sugar, and bake in a cool oven until lightly browned. Serve either hot or cold.

There are two ways of making a flan without the aid of a ring. The first is by means of a round cake-tin. The tin is placed in the centre of the rolled-out paste, which is cut round, leaving a margin of about 1 inch, to be afterwards raised and moulded to the shape of the tin. Before removing the tin a narrow-folded band of greased paper must be pinned lightly round this raised border. In the second method, the bottom is cut out to the required size, and a narrow strip of paste fastened to the edge of it by means of white of egg. A band of paper must support the border ; and in both cases the inside should be filled with rice before baking.

FLAN OF PINEAPPLE.

Procure ½ a preserved pineapple, castor sugar, 2 eggs, and ½ a lb. of short-crust paste (p. 87). Sufficient for 5 or 6 persons.

Prepare and bake the flan as for **Flan of Apples.** Cut the pineapple into dice and remove all the specks. Strain the syrup, place a ¼-pint of it in a stewpan with a dessertspoonful of sugar, bring to boiling-point, and simmer for 3 or 4 minutes. Let it cool slightly, then add the yolks of the eggs, and cook gently by the side of the fire until they thicken, stirring meanwhile. Now place the pineapple in the prepared flan, cover with the custard, and spread the stiffly-whisked whites of eggs on the top. Bake in a moderately cool oven until the méringue hardens, and browns slightly. Serve either hot or cold.

FLAN OF STRAWBERRIES.

With 1 lb. of strawberries, take castor sugar, 2 whites of eggs, and ½ a lb. of short-crust paste (p. 87). Sufficient for 5 or 6 persons.

Make the flan as directed for **Flan of Apples** (p. 95); when about ¾ baked remove the rice, and fill with strawberries, from which the stalks have been removed. Pile the fruit high in the centre, dredge well with castor sugar, and cover with stiffly-whisked white of egg. Cover the surface lightly with castor sugar, replace in the oven, and bake slowly for about 15 minutes. When the méringue is set, cover with paper to prevent it browning too much before the strawberries are sufficiently cooked. Serve either hot or cold.

Note.—Almost any kind of fruit may be made into a flan; the varieties employed for culinary purposes may be broadly divided into 3 classes, viz., fruit requiring a comparatively large amount of cooking, such as apples, pears, plums; quickly-cooked fruits like strawberries, raspberries, etc.; and tinned fruits which simply require re-heating. The 3 preceding recipes illustrate methods applicable in each case.

FOLKESTONE CHEESECAKES.

To 1 pint of milk, allow 4 oz. of sugar, 3 oz. of ground rice, 2 oz. of butter, 2 oz. of currants cleaned, 2 eggs, the grated rind of ½ a lemon, salt, and short-crust paste (p. 87). Sufficient for 12 large cheesecakes.

Simmer the ground rice in the milk for ¼ of an hour, stir in the butter, sugar, lemon-rind, the well-beaten eggs, a good pinch of salt, and stir and cook by the side of the fire until the mixture thickens. Now let it cool slightly, and meanwhile line the patty-pans with paste, and unless the oven has a good bottom heat, half bake them before putting in the mixture (*see* **Cherry Tartlets**, p. 92). When ready, fill them with the cheesecake preparation, sprinkle a few currants on the top of each cake, and bake from 25 to 30 minutes in a brisk oven.

FRUIT OR JAM TURNOVERS.

Have ready some short-crust or puff-paste (p. 85), stewed fruit or jam, and castor sugar.

ICES

1. Ice Pudding.　　　2. Dessert Ices.

1. Neapolitan Ices. 2. Grape Sorbets. 3. Nesselrode Pudding.

Roll the paste out thinly, and cut it into rounds about 4 inches in diameter. Place a little fruit or jam in the centre of each round, moisten the edges with water, and fold the paste over on 3 sides in the form of a triangle. Seal the join carefully, turn them over, brush lightly with cold water, and dredge well with castor sugar. Bake in a moderate oven for about 15 minutes.

GOOSEBERRY TART.

To 1½ pints of gooseberries, allow ¼ of a lb. of short-crust paste (p. 87), and ¼ of a lb. of moist sugar. Sufficient for 5 or 6 persons.

With a pair of scissors cut off the tops and tails of the gooseberries ; put them into a deep pie-dish, pile the fruit high in the centre, and put in the sugar ; line the edge of the dish with short-crust, put on the cover, and ornament the edges of the tart ; bake in a good oven for about ¾ of an hour, and before serving dredge with castor sugar.

GRANVILLE TARTLETS.

Take 3 oz. of castor sugar, 2 oz. of butter, 2 oz. of currants cleaned and picked, 1 oz. of ground rice, 1 oz. of finely-shredded candied peel, 3 oz. of cake-crumbs, 1 oz. of desiccated coco-nut, 2 whites of eggs, 1 tablespoonful of cream (optional), lemon-essence, and some short-crust paste (p. 87), and transparent icing (p. 104). Sufficient for 18 tartlets.

Cream the butter and sugar together until thick and smooth, add the currants, ground rice, peel, cake-crumbs, cream (if used), 4 or 5 drops of lemon-essence, and lastly, the stiffiy-whisked whites of eggs. Line 18 small oval tartlet moulds with paste, fill them with the preparation, and bake from 15 to 20 minutes in a moderate oven. When cool, mask the tartlets with icing, and sprinkle them with desiccated coco-nut.

LEMON CHEESECAKES.

Make sufficient short-crust paste (p. 87) to line about 30 patty-pans, and take 1 lb. of loaf sugar, ¼ of a lb. of butter, 3 eggs, the grated rind of 2 lemons and the juice of 3, and finely-shredded candied peel.

Put the sugar, butter, lemon-rind and strained lemon-juice into a stewpan, and stir until the sugar is dissolved. Beat the eggs, add them to the contents of the stewpan, and stir and cook slowly until the mixture thickens. Let it remain in a cool dry place until required. Line the patty-pans with paste, three parts fill them with the preparation, add a few strips of candied peel, and bake for about 20 minutes in a moderately hot oven.

Note.—The above preparation, if closely covered and stored in a cool, dry place, will keep good for several weeks.

LEMON TARTLETS.

Take 4 oz. of butter, 4 oz. of castor sugar, 2 eggs, and 1 lemon, and prepare sufficient short-crust paste (p. 87) to line about 18 patty-pans.

Cream the butter and sugar well together, beat each egg in separately, and add the juice of the lemon and the rind finely grated. Let the mixture stand in a cool, dry place for at least 24 hours, then bake in patty-pans, previously lined with the short-crust paste (from 15 to 20 minutes).

MAIDS OF HONOUR.

Prepare sufficient puff-paste (p. 85) to line 8 or 9 patty-pans, and take 4 oz. of castor-sugar, 2 oz. of Jordan almonds, ½ an oz. of fine flour, 1 egg, 2 tablespoonfuls of cream, and 1 tablespoonful of orange-flower water.

Blanch and dry the almonds, and pound them in a mortar with the sugar until fine. Add the egg, and mix in the flour, cream and orange-flower water. Line 8 or 9 small tartlet moulds with paste, fill them with the mixture, and bake in a moderate oven for about 15 minutes.

MÉRINGUE TARTS.   (*See* **Flan of Apples,** p. 95; **Flan of Strawberries,** p. 96; **Apple Amber,** p. 89.)

MINCE PIES.

Make some puff-paste (p. 85), and procure or make some mincemeat (p. 103).

When the paste has had the necessary number of turns, roll it out to about a ¼ of an inch in thickness, and line some large-sized patty-pans with it. Fill with mincemeat, cover with paste, brush over lightly with cold water, and dredge with castor sugar. Bake in a moderately hot oven from 25 to 30 minutes, and serve either hot or cold.

OPEN TART. (Of any kind of Preserve.)

Have ready some trimmings of puff-paste, and any kind of jam.

Butter a tart-pan of the usual shape, roll out the paste to the thickness of ⅛ of an inch, and line the pan with it, prick a few holes at the bottom with a fork to prevent the paste rising and blistering, and bake the tart in a brisk oven from 10 to 15 minutes. Let the paste cool a little ; then fill it with preserve, place on it a few stars or leaves, which have been previously cut out of paste and baked, and the tart is ready for table. By making the tart in this manner, both the flavour and the colour of the jam are preserved.

PASTRY SANDWICHES.

Take some pastry trimmings, jam, and castor sugar.

Knead the trimmings lightly into a smooth round ball, and roll out very thinly, keeping the shape as square as possible. Spread jam evenly over one half, fold the other half over, wet the edges, and press them lightly together. Brush over with water, dredge well with castor sugar, and with the back of a blade of a knife mark the paste across in lines about 1 inch apart. Bake for about 20 minutes in a moderate oven, and when cold cut the paste into strips. If preferred, currants, with the addition of a little sugar and shredded candied peel, may be used instead of jam.

PUFF TARTLETS.

Have ready some puff-paste trimmings, jam, white of egg, and castor sugar.

Roll the paste out to about a ¼ of an inch in thickness, and stamp out an equal number of rounds, 2½ and 1¾ inches in diameter. Brush the larger rounds over with white of egg ; stamp out the centre of the smaller rounds, thus forming them into rings, one of which must be pressed lightly on the top of each round of paste. Bake for about 15 minutes in a moderately hot oven, and when cold fill with jam.

RASPBERRY TARTLETS.

Prepare sufficient short-crust paste (p. 87), to line about 12 patty-pans, and take 1 pint of raspberries, ½ a lb. of loaf sugar, ¼ of a pint of water, ½ a glass of brandy (optional), and desiccated coco-nut.

Boil the sugar and water together until reduced to a syrup, add the raspberries, and cook gently for a few minutes. Drain, replace the syrup in the stewpan, boil rapidly until considerably reduced, then let it cool, and add the brandy (if used). Line 10 or 12 patty-pans with paste, fill them with rice placed in buttered papers, and bake in a moderately hot oven until crisp (10 to 15 minutes). When cool, fill them with the prepared fruit, and an equal portion of syrup to each tartlet, sprinkle with coco-nut, and serve cold.

RED-CURRANT AND RASPBERRY TART.

With 1½ pints of red-currants and ½ a pint of raspberries, take 2 or 3 tablespoonfuls of moist sugar and some short-crust paste (p. 87).

Strip the currants from the stalks, put half of them into a pie-dish with an inverted cup in the midst, add the sugar and raspberries, then the remainder of the currants, piling them rather high in the centre. Cover with paste (*see* **Apple Tart**), brush lightly over with water, dredge well with castor sugar, and bake for about ¾ of an hour in a moderately hot oven.

ST. CLOUD TARTLETS.

Have ready some short-crust paste (p. 87), puff-paste or puff-paste trimmings, ½ a lb. of greengage jam, castor sugar, vanilla sugar, ½ a gill of cream, glacé cherries, beaten egg or water, a little milk, and angelica. Sufficient for 8 or 9 tartlets.

Line the patty-pans with short-paste, brush the edges lightly over with beaten egg or water, and sprinkle with castor sugar. Fill them with jam, and bake in a moderately hot oven from 10 to 15 minutes. Roll the puff-paste out to about ⅛ of an inch in thickness, and stamp out some rings fully ½ an inch less in diameter than the tartlets. Brush them over with milk, turn the wet side on to the castor sugar, and place on the baking-sheet sugared side upwards. Bake in a quick oven ; when cold, place the rings of paste on the tartlets, and fill the centre with cream stiffly whipped and sweetened with vanilla sugar. Place half a glacé cherry in the centre of each, and insert a few strips or leaves of angelica to complete the decoration.

CHAPTER VIII

ICINGS AND FILLINGS FOR COLD SWEETS

ALMOND PASTE.

To 4 oz. of ground almonds, allow 6 oz. of loaf sugar, 1 white of egg, and a teaspoonful of lemon-juice.

Put the sugar, with 1 tablespoonful of water, and the lemon-juice into a stewpan, bring to the boil, skim well, and boil to the " small ball " degree (237° F.). Pour the syrup on to the ground almonds, add about half the white of egg, mix well together, and use as required.

CHOCOLATE ICING.

Take 3 oz. of chocolate, ½ a lb. of icing sugar, and ¼ a gill of water. Sufficient for icing a small cake.

Break the chocolate into small pieces, put them into a small stewpan with the water, and stir by the side of the fire until dissolved. Add the icing sugar, stir until well mixed and smooth, then use as required.

COFFEE BUTTER.

With ¼ of a lb. of fresh butter, take ¼ of a lb. of castor sugar, 1 yolk of egg, and coffee essence. Sufficient for decorating a small cake.

Cream the sugar and yolk of egg for about 10 minutes, add coffee essence to taste, and the softened butter gradually. Work until thoroughly mixed and smooth, let it remain on ice until firm, stir again, then use for decorating, by means of a paper cornet, or bag and forcer.

COFFEE ICING.

Have ready 1 lb. of icing sugar or fine castor sugar, 1 gill of cold water, and 1 dessertspoonful of coffee essence.

Put the sugar and water into a stewpan, stir by the side of the fire until it reaches boiling-point, and simmer for 4 or 5 minutes. Pour the syrup into a basin, add the coffee essence, and stir until the icing becomes less transparent as it cools. If used before it reaches this point it will have a dull appearance.

CONFECTIONER'S CUSTARD.

Procure 4 yolks of eggs, 1½ pints of milk, 4 oz. of castor sugar, ½ an oz. of potato flour, 3 sheets of gelatine, and flavouring essence. Sufficient for 1½ pints of custard.

Mix the potato flour smoothly with a little milk, boil the remainder, add the sugar and blended potato flour, boil for 2 minutes, then pour over the beaten yolks of eggs, stirring meanwhile. Return to the stewpan and stir by the side of the fire until the mixture thickens, then add the gelatine, previously dissolved in 1 tablespoonful of water, and the flavouring essence, and use as required.

FRANGIPAN CREAM.

With ½ a lb. of fine sifted flour, take ¼ of a lb. of castor sugar, 2 oz. of butter, 2 eggs, 1 pint of milk, flavouring essence, and a pinch of salt. Sufficient to fill 12 tartlets.

Put the eggs, the flour, sugar, and a little pinch of salt into a small stewpan, stir and cook by the side of the fire until well mixed, then add the milk gradually. When perfectly smooth, stir in the butter, cook gently for about 10 minutes, then turn into a basin, flavour to taste, and when cool use as required for filling tartlets, etc.

MINCEMEAT.

Have ready 1 lb. of finely-chopped suet, 1 lb. of currants washed and picked, 1 lb. of raisins stoned and quartered, 1 lb. of chopped apples, 1 lb. of castor sugar, ½ a lb. of sultanas, ¼ of a lb. of shredded mixed candied peel, 2 lemons, ½ a gill of brandy, ½ a saltspoonful each of nutmeg, mace and cinnamon. Sufficient for 4 or 5 lb. of mincemeat.

Pare the lemons thinly, simmer the rinds in a little water until perfectly tender, then pound them or rub them through a fine sieve. Mix all the ingredients well together, press into a jar, cover closely, and keep in a cool, dry place for at least 1 month before using.

MINCEMEAT. (Another Method.)

Take 1 lb. of finely-chopped apples, 1 lb. of currants cleaned and picked, ¾ of a lb. of finely-chopped suet, ¾ of a lb. of raisins, stoned and quartered, ¾ of a lb. of castor sugar, ¼ of a lb. of finely-shredded mixed candied peel, the grated rind and juice of 2 lemons, ½ a teaspoonful of cinnamon, ground cloves, mace and nutmeg, mixed in equal proportions, and ¼ of a pint of brandy. Sufficient for 4 or 5 lb. of mincemeat.

Mix all these ingredients well together, press them into a jar, cover closely and store in a cool, dry place until required. It should be kept for 1 month at least before being used.

MINCEMEAT (Economical.)

With 1 lb. of chopped apples, take ¾ of a lb. of currants washed and picked, ½ a lb. of raisins stoned and quartered, ½ a lb. of finely-chopped suet, ½ a lb. of castor sugar, 2 oz. of chopped candied peel, the juice and grated rind of 1 lemon, and 1 saltspoonful of grated nutmeg. Sufficient for 3 or 4 lb. of mincemeat.

Mix all these ingredients well together, and keep in closely-covered jars in a cool, dry place, until required.

MINCEMEAT, LEMON.

Take 2 large lemons, 6 large apples, ½ a lb. of suet, 1 lb. of currants, ½ a lb. of sugar, 2 oz. of candied lemon-peel, 1 oz. of citron, and mixed spice to taste. Sufficient for 2 or 3 lb. of mincemeat.

Pare the lemons, squeeze them, and boil the peel until it is tender enough to mash. Add to the mashed lemon-peel the apples, which should be pared, cored and minced, the chopped suet, currants, sugar, sliced peel and spice. Strain the lemon-juice to these ingredients, stir the mixture well, and put it in a jar with a close-fitting lid. Stir occasionally, and in a week or 10 days the mincemeat will be ready for use.

MOKA CUSTARD FOR FILLING ÉCLAIRS.

With 1 gill of milk, take 1 oz. of loaf sugar, ½ an oz. of cornflour, ½ an oz. of fresh butter, 1 egg, 1 teaspoonful of coffee essence and a few drops of vanilla essence.

Put the milk and sugar in a stewpan to boil. Mix the cornflour with a little cold milk, pour the boiling milk on this, mix thoroughly, return to the stewpan, and let it boil for a few minutes, add the flavouring essences and the butter, stir in the egg, continue to stir until the mixture binds, pour it in a basin, and let it cool.

ORANGE ICING.

Have ready 6 oz. of icing sugar and the juice of 1 orange. Sufficient for 10 or 12 tartlets.

Put the sugar and orange-juice into a small stewpan, stir until well mixed and smooth, and pour an equal portion over the top of each tartlet.

ROYAL ICING.

To ½ a lb. of icing sugar, allow 1 teaspoonful of lemon-juice and 1 white of egg. Sufficient to ice 6 or 8 tartlets.

Put the white of egg into a basin, add the sugar gradually and work well with a wooden spoon. When the preparation presents a smooth, white brilliant appearance, add the lemon-juice, and use as required.

TRANSPARENT ICING.

Procure 1 lb. of loaf sugar and ½ a gill of warm water. Sufficient to ice a small cake.

Put the sugar and water into a sugar boiler or stewpan, let it dissolve, then bring to the boil and simmer for about 5 minutes, or until a thick syrup is formed (230° Fahr. on a saccharometer). Pour into a basin, stir until almost cold and setting, then use as required.

VANILLA SUGAR.

Take 2 lb. of castor sugar and 1 oz. of vanilla pod.

Cut the pod into small pieces, pound with the sugar in a mortar until smooth, then rub through a fine sieve. Unless kept in a perfectly air-tight tin, the sugar will lose much of its flavour.

CHAPTER IX

ICES

Cream Ices

ALMOND CREAM ICE.

Have ready 3 oz. of sweet almonds, 3 bitter almonds, ½ a pint of custard (p. 109), ¼ of a pint of whipped cream, ¼ of a pint of milk, a few drops of almond essence, and 1 teaspoonful of orange-flower water. Sufficient for 5 or 6 persons.

Blanch, chop and pound the almonds smoothly, adding the orange-flower water to prevent them oiling. Warm the milk, pour it over the almonds, let it remain covered while the custard is made and gets cold, then mix the whole together. Partially freeze, then add the cream, almond essence, sugar if necessary, and complete the freezing.

APRICOT ICED EGGS.

With 12 apricots (preserved ones will serve), take 4 oz. of castor sugar, 1 pint of cream, the juice of 1 lemon, and 2 or 3 drops of carmine. Allow 1 egg mould for each person.

Pass the fruit through a hair sieve, stir in the sugar and lemon-juice, and add the cream stiffly whipped. Mix in a little carmine, freeze, press lightly into egg moulds, and pack in ice until required.

BANANA CREAM ICE.

Prepare 1¼ pints of Custard No. 1 (p. 109), and take ¼ of a pint of cream, 6 bananas, and 1 tablespoonful of lemon-juice. Sufficient for 7 or 8 persons.

Pass the bananas through a fine hair sieve. Prepare the custard as directed, and whip the cream stiffly. When the custard is sufficiently cool, add the banana pulp and lemon-juice, stir in lightly the cream, and freeze in the usual manner (*see* p. 13).

BISCUIT ICE CREAM.

Make some ice cream, and procure some savoy biscuits. A pint mould should be sufficient for 4 or 5 persons.

Line a plain ice mould with savoy biscuits, put in the frozen cream ice, cover, and pack in ice until required.

BROWN BREAD CREAM ICE.

Take 1 pint of Custard No. 1 or 2 (p. 109), 3 oz. of crumbled brown bread, and ½ a gill of cream. Sufficient for 5 or 6 persons.

Pass the brown bread through a sieve, and bake in a cool oven until crisp and well browned. Partially freeze the custard, add the brown crumbs and cream, complete the freezing and mould.

BURNT ALMOND CREAM.

With 1½ pints of Custard No. 1 (p. 109), take ¾ of a gill of cream, 1 tablespoonful of Kirsch (optional), 2 oz. of loaf sugar, and 2 oz. of almonds. Sufficient for 7 or 8 persons.

Blanch, shred, and bake the almonds until brown, prepare the custard according to the recipe. Put the sugar and a few drops of water into a small stewpan, and boil until it acquires a deep golden-brown colour. Now add the cream, boil up and stir into the custard. Let the mixture cool, then add the prepared almonds and Kirsch (if used), and freeze in the usual manner.

CARAMEL CREAM ICE.

To 1½ pints of Custard No. 1 (p. 109), allow ¾ of a gill of cream, and 2 oz. of loaf sugar. Sufficient for about 7 or 8 persons.

Prepare the custard as directed. Put the sugar into a small stewpan with a few drops of water, and boil until it acquires a deep golden-brown colour. Now add the cream, and when boiling stir into the custard. Let the mixture cool, then freeze.

CHERRY CREAM ICE.

Make 1 pint of Custard No. 2 (p. 109), and take ¾ of a lb. of ripe cherries, 2 oz. of castor sugar, the juice of 1 lemon, 1 tablespoonful of liqueur, and carmine. Sufficient for 7 or 8 persons.

Stone the fruit, crack the stones, take out the kernels, place both cherries and kernels in a basin, add the sugar, lemon-juice, liqueur, cover, and let the preparation stand for ½ an hour. Then pour all into a copper stewpan, add ½ a pint of water, cook until the cherries are tender, and rub through a fine sieve. Add the prepared custard and a few drops of carmine, and freeze as directed (*see* instructions on p. 13).

CHOCOLATE BOMBE, WITH FRUIT.

Prepare a bomb of chocolate cream ice as per instructions given in the following recipe, and fill the interior with cream sweetened, slightly stiffened with gelatine, and mixed with halved or quartered strawberries.

CHOCOLATE CREAM ICE.

Have ready 4 oz. of chocolate, 1 pint of Custard No. 1 or 2 (p. 109), 1 gill of milk, ½ a gill of cream, and sugar to taste. Sufficient for 7 or 8 persons.

Prepare the custard as directed. Dissolve the chocolate in the milk, sweeten to taste, and strain it into the custard. Let the mixture cool, then add the stiffly-whipped cream, and freeze (*see* p. 13).

CIDER ICE.

With 1 pint of cider, take 1 pint of syrup (p. 46), ½ a pint of unsweetened apple pulp, and the juice of 3 lemons. Sufficient for 6 or 7 persons.

Mix all the ingredients together, boil up, pass through a fine sieve, and, when cold, freeze as directed (*see* p. 13). The ice may be coloured pale green or pink by adding a few drops of either spinach extract or carmine.

CLARIFIED SUGAR FOR WATER ICE. (*See* Syrup for Water Ices, p. 118.)

COCOA ICED. (*See* Coffee Iced, p. 119.)

COFFEE CREAM ICE.

Procure 1½ oz. of freshly-roasted and ground coffee, 3 oz. of castor sugar, 1 pint of Custard No. 1 or 2 (p. 109), and ½ a gill of cream. Sufficient for 7 or 8 persons.

Pour boiling water over the coffee, infuse for about ½ an hour, then strain, add the sugar, and let it cool. Make the custard according to the recipe, stir in the coffee ; when cool, add the whipped cream, and freeze (*see* p. 13).

COFFEE CREAM ICE. (Another Method.)

Prepare 1 pint of very strong clear coffee, and take 1¼ pints of cream and 4 oz. of castor sugar. Sufficient for about 7 or 8 persons.

Sweeten the coffee with the sugar, partially freeze it, then stir in the slightly-whipped cream, and continue the freezing (*see* p. 13).

COFFEE SAUCE FOR CREAM ICE.

Take 6 tablespoonfuls of freshly-ground coffee, ¾ of a pint of boiling water, 3 oz. of castor sugar, 3 yolks of eggs, and 2 sheets of gelatine. Sufficient to make 1 pint of sauce.

Pour the boiling water over the coffee, let it stand until clear, then strain it into a saucepan. Beat the yolks of eggs and sugar together, and dissolve the gelatine in a very little cold water. Add both to the coffee, stir and cook slowly until the preparation has the consistency of thick cream, then strain, and serve separately when cold.

CREAM ICE (en Surprise).

Moulded cream ice, masked with méringue, and quickly baked.

CREAM ICE FROM FRESH FRUIT.

With 1 pint of milk, take ½ a pint of cream, ½ a pint of fruit pulp, sugar to taste, the juice of 1 lemon, and the white of 1 egg. Sufficient for 7 or 8 persons.

Put the milk and sugar into a stewpan, bring to the boil and cool. Pass the fruit through a fine hair sieve, add the lemon-juice and milk to the pulp thus formed, and stir in lightly the stiffly-whipped cream. When the mixture is partially frozen, add the well-whisked white of egg, and continue the freezing.

Note.—In a recipe of this description the exact amount of sugar cannot be stated. It varies with the fruit ; but it must be added with discretion, for if the mixture is made too sweet, freezing is extremely difficult, while, on the other hand, if not sufficiently sweetened the ice becomes too solid.

CREAM ICES FROM PRESERVED FRUIT OR JAM.

To 1 pint of milk, allow 1 gill of cream, 3 yolks of eggs, sugar to taste, and 6 oz. of preserved fruit pulp or jam, such as strawberry, raspberry, greengage, apricot, peach, pineapple, etc. Sufficient for 7 or 8 persons.

Beat the yolks of eggs, add the milk when nearly boiling, replace in the stewpan, and stir by the side of the fire until they thicken, but the mixture must not boil. Strain, add the sieved jam or fruit pulp, sweeten to taste and brighten the colour by adding a few drops of carmine, saffron, or spinach greening, according to the fruit used. Let the preparation cool, then add the stiffly-whipped cream, and freeze as directed.

CUSTARD (for Cream Ices) No. 1.

Have ready 1 pint of milk, $\frac{1}{4}$ of a pint of cream, 4 oz. of castor sugar, and 4 yolks of eggs. Sufficient to make about $1\frac{3}{4}$ pints of custard.

Bring the milk nearly to boiling-point, and pour it over the beaten yolks of eggs, stirring meanwhile. Return to the stewpan, and stir by the side of the fire until the mixture thickens, but do not let it boil, or the eggs may curdle. Stir in the sugar, strain, and when cool add the cream.

CUSTARD (for Cream Ices) No. 2.

Take $1\frac{1}{2}$ pints of milk, 1 gill of cream, 6 oz. of castor sugar, 1 heaped dessertspoonful of cornflour, and 2 or 3 eggs. Sufficient to make about $1\frac{3}{4}$ pints of custard.

Mix the cornflour smoothly with a little milk, boil the remainder with the sugar, add the blended cornflour and milk, and simmer for 3 or 4 minutes. Cool slightly, then add the beaten yolks of eggs, and stir by the side of the fire until the mixture thickens. Strain into a basin ; when cool add the cream, the whites of eggs stiffly whisked, and use as required.

CUSTARD (for Cream Ices) No. 3.

With $1\frac{1}{2}$ pints of milk, take 6 oz. of castor sugar, $\frac{1}{2}$ an oz. of cornflour, and saffron-yellow colouring. Sufficient to make about $1\frac{1}{2}$ pints of custard.

Mix the cornflour smoothly with a little milk, boil the remainder with the sugar, add the blended cornflour and milk, and simmer gently for 3 or 4 minutes. Strain, add sufficient colouring matter to give the mixture the appearance of rich custard, and use as required.

FIG CREAM ICE.

Have ready 1 breakfastcupful of finely-chopped dried figs, 2 oz. of castor sugar, 1 dessertspoonful of best isinglass, 2 tablespoonfuls of cornflour, a little vanilla essence, 1 quart of milk, 1 pint of cream, and 2 or 3 eggs. Sufficient for from 10 to 12 persons.

Mix the cornflour smoothly with a little milk, boil the remainder, add the cornflour, and stir until boiling. Beat the eggs and sugar together, stir them into the milk and cornflour, add the isinglass previously softened in a little cold water, and stir it until dissolved. When cold, add the cream and a little vanilla essence, freeze slightly, then add the figs and complete the freezing operation (see instructions on p. 13).

FREEZING ICE CREAM IN A REFRIGERATOR.
(See p. 14.)

FRUIT CREAM ICE.

To ½ a pint of fresh fruit pulp (strawberry, raspberry, or any other fruit), allow 8 oz. of sugar, ½ a pint of cream, 1 pint of milk, the juice of 1 lemon, and the stiffly-whisked white of 1 egg. This should be sufficient for from 10 to 12 persons.

Boil the milk, add the sugar, and put aside until nearly cold. Obtain the pulp by passing the fruit through a fine hair sieve, add the lemon-juice, milk, and the cream stiffly whipped. Partially freeze the preparation before adding the white of egg. The amount of sugar required depends upon the fruit used.

GINGER ICE CREAM.

Prepare 1½ pints of Custard No. 1, 2 or 3 (p. 109), and take 3 oz. of preserved ginger, and 1 teaspoonful of ginger syrup. Sufficient for 7 or 8 persons.

Make the custard as directed. Cut the ginger into small dice, stir it with the syrup into the custard, and freeze (see p. 13).

ICE PUDDING. (*See* **Iced Queen's Pudding,** p. 120, and **Nesselrode Pudding,** p. 122.)

ICED SOUFFLÉ. (*See* **Strawberry or Raspberry Soufflé, Iced,** p. 124.)

JAPANESE PLOMBIÈRE.

With 6 yolks of eggs, take 1 oz. of sugar, 4 oz. of ground almonds, ½ a pint of cream, 1½ pints of milk, apricot marmalade, 4 oz. of pounded macaroons, salt, and ratafias or ice wafers. Sufficient for from 8 to 10 persons.

Boil up the milk, pour it over the yolks of eggs, add a little salt and the sugar, and replace in the saucepan. Cook gently for a few minutes, then tammy or pass through a fine hair sieve, and add 2 oz. of marmalade, and the almonds. When cold, add the macaroons and the cream stiffly whipped, and freeze. Mould with a little apricot marmalade in the centre, and serve garnished with ratafias or ice wafers.

LEMON CREAM ICE.

Make 1 pint of Custard No. 1, 2 or 3 (p. 109), and take 4 oz. of loaf sugar, and 2 lemons. Sufficient for 7 or 8 persons.

Prepare the custard as directed. Rub the lumps of sugar on the rinds of the lemons until all the outer yellow part is removed, and dissolve it in 1 tablespoonful of warm water. Add the juice of 1 lemon, and when cool stir into the custard. If necessary, add a few drops of liquid saffron colouring, and freeze.

MAPLE PARFAIT.

Take 1½ gills of thick syrup, 1 quart of cream, 4 oz. of maple sugar, 3 yolks of eggs, and 1 inch of vanilla pod. Sufficient for 9 or 10 persons.

Boil the syrup and vanilla pod in a copper pan until it registers 240° on a saccharometer, then remove the vanilla, and pour the syrup over the yolks of eggs previously well beaten. Whisk the preparation in an egg-bowl over boiling water until it has the consistency of thick cream, and afterwards whisk until cold. Add the stiffly-whipped cream and maple sugar, stir for some minutes over the ice, then turn into a parfait or bomb mould lined with paper. Secure and seal the lid, and imbed in ice from 2½ to 3 hours.

ORANGE ICE CREAM.

Prepare 1½ pints of Custard No. **1, 2 or 3** (p. 109), and take 3 oranges, 2 oz. of loaf sugar, saffron-yellow colouring, and carmine. Sufficient for 7 or 8 persons.

Prepare the custard as directed. Remove the outer yellow part of 2 oranges by rubbing them with the lumps of sugar, which afterwards must be dissolved in 1 tablespoonful of warm water. Mix with the strained juice of the oranges; when cool stir into the custard, and add the carmine and saffron-yellow, until the desired colour is obtained. Freeze as directed on p. 13.

PINEAPPLE CREAM ICE.

To 1 pint of Custard No. 1 or 2 (p. 109), allow ½ a lb. of finely-chopped preserved pineapple, ½ a gill of pineapple syrup, and 1 teaspoonful of lemon-juice. Sufficient for 7 or 8 persons.

Pass the pineapple through a fine sieve, and mix with it the syrup and lemon-juice. Make the custard as directed, and when cool stir in the pineapple preparation, and freeze as directed (p. 13).

PINEAPPLE PLOMBIÈRE.

With 1 quart of cream, take 4 yolks of eggs, 4 oz. of sugar, 3 tablespoonfuls of pineapple dice, 3 tablespoonfuls of pine-apple syrup, and vanilla essence. Sufficient for 10 or more persons.

Boil up 1½ pints of the cream, pour it over the yolks of eggs previously well beaten, add the sugar and pineapple syrup, and replace the mixture in the saucepan. Stir and cook gently by the side of the fire for a few minutes, then strain, and, when cold, freeze. When the mixture is half frozen, add the pineapple dice, a little vanilla essence, and the remaining cream stiffly whipped.

PISTACHIO CREAM ICE.

Have ready 1½ pints of Custard No. 1, 2 or 3 (p. 109), 4 oz. of pistachio nuts blanched and pounded, 1 tablespoonful of noyeau, orange-flower water, and spinach-greening. Sufficient for 7 or 8 persons.

While pounding the pistachio nuts add gradually a little

orange-flower water. As soon as the custard is cold, add the noyeau and a little spinach extract, and when partially frozen stir in the pistachio nuts.

RASPBERRY ICE CREAM.

To 1 lb. of raspberries, allow 1 pint of Custard No. 1, 2 or 3 (p. 109), 4 to 6 oz. of castor sugar, 1 teaspoonful of lemon-juice, and carmine. Sufficient for 7 or 8 persons.

Make the custard as directed. Pass the raspberries through a fine hair sieve, add the sugar and lemon-juice, and mix with the prepared custard, adding at the same time as much carmine as is needed to produce a bright red colour. Freeze as directed, *see* instructions on p. 13.

STRAWBERRY ICE CREAM.

With 1 lb. of strawberries, take ½ a pint of cream, ¼ of a pint of milk, 1 or 2 yolks of eggs, 6 oz. of castor sugar, 1 teaspoonful of lemon-juice, and carmine. Sufficient for 7 or 8 persons.

Bring the milk and cream to near boiling-point, add the beaten yolks of eggs, stir by the side of the fire until they thicken, then put in the sugar, and when dissolved, strain and let the preparation cool. Pass the strawberries through a fine sieve, mix with the custard, add the lemon-juice and carmine gradually until a deep pink colour is obtained. Freeze as directed on p. 13.

STRAWBERRY ICE CREAM. (Another Method.)

Procure 1 lb. of strawberries, 1 quart of milk, ½ a gill of cream, 6 oz. of castor sugar, ½ an oz. of cornflour, 2 or 3 eggs, the juice of 2 lemons, and carmine. Sufficient for 7 or 8 persons.

Mix the cornflour with a little milk, boil the remainder with the sugar, add the blended cornflour and milk, simmer for 2 or 3 minutes, then cool slightly. Beat the yolks of the eggs, add them to the contents of the stewpan, and stir by the side of the fire until the mixture thickens. Strain, add the strawberries previously reduced to a purée by being passed through a fine sieve, the lemon-juice, a few drops of carmine, and when cold, the cream and well-whisked whites of eggs. Freeze the mixture in the usual manner (*see* instructions given on p. 13).

C.S. H

TEA CREAM ICE.

Prepare ½ a pint of strong tea and 1 pint of Custard No. 2 (p. 109), and take 1 tablespoonful of thick cream, and 2 oz. of castor sugar. Sufficient for 7 or 8 persons.

Strain the tea, add the sugar, and let it cool. Prepare the custard as directed, add the tea ; when cool, stir in the cream, and freeze in the usual manner.

TEA ICE CREAM, AMERICAN.

To 1 pint of milk, allow 2 tablespoonfuls of dry tea, ½ a pint of cream, 6 oz. of castor sugar, 2 whole eggs, and 1 inch of vanilla pod. Sufficient for 7 or 8 persons.

Bring the milk and vanilla pod to boiling-point, infuse for a few minutes, then pour it over the tea, allow it to remain closely covered for 5 minutes, and strain. Beat the eggs well, add the castor sugar, and continue the beating until perfectly smooth, then stir in the prepared tea. Put this mixture into a stewpan, and stir by the side of the fire until it thickens. Strain into a basin ; when cool, add the stiffly-whipped cream and freeze in the usual manner.

TUTTI-FRUTTI, ICED (MIXED FRUIT ICE).

Take 1 oz. of pistachios blanched and shredded, 1 oz. of glacé cherries, 1 oz. of glacé apricots, ½ an oz. of mixed candied peel, all cut into small dice, ½ a pint of cream stiffly whipped, ½ a gill of Maraschino (optional), 2 whites of eggs stiffly whisked, vanilla essence, 4 oz. of sugar, 3 yolks of eggs, and 1 pint of milk. Sufficient for 8 or 9 persons.

Boil the milk, add the yolks of eggs and sugar, stir and cook very gently for a few minutes, then strain and, when cold, add vanilla essence to taste. Partially freeze, add the whites of eggs, cream, nuts and fruit, and, when the freezing process is nearly completed, put in the Maraschino (if liked).

VANILLA ICE CREAM.

Have ready 1 pint of cream, ½ a pint of milk, 4 oz. of castor sugar, 4 yolks of eggs, and ½ a pod of vanilla. Sufficient for 7 or 8 persons.

Whisk the yolks of eggs and sugar well together, boil the cream and milk with the vanilla for a few minutes, stir into the eggs, etc., and replace the whole in the stewpan. Stir by the side of the fire until the mixture thickens, but it must on no account be allowed to boil. Tammy or pass through a fine strainer if necessary, add a few drops of vanilla essence, and when cool, freeze in the usual manner.

VANILLA ICE CREAM. (Economical.)

With 1½ pints of milk, take 4 oz. of castor sugar, ½ an oz. of cornflour, and ½ a teaspoonful of vanilla essence, saffron or liquid yellow colouring. Sufficient for 6 or 7 persons.

Mix the cornflour smoothly with a little milk, boil the remainder with the sugar, add the blended cornflour and milk, and simmer gently for 2 minutes. Strain; when cool, add the vanilla essence and sufficient colouring matter to give the mixture the appearance of rich custard. Freeze as directed.

VANILLA PLOMBIÈRE.

Prepare 1½ pints of vanilla ice cream mixture (p. 114), ½ a pint of stiffly-whipped cream, and 2 tablespoonfuls of coarsely-chopped almonds.

Partially freeze the vanilla ice cream, add the whipped cream and almonds, and complete the freezing, *see* instructions on p. 13.

WALNUT CREAM ICE. (*See* Pistachio Cream Ice, p. 112.)

Omit the spinach-greening, and, if preferred, substitute vanilla essence for the noyeau.

WATER ICES

APPLE WATER ICE.

Have ready 1 pint of apple pulp, 1 pint of syrup (p. 118), and 2 tablespoonfuls of lemon-juice. Sufficient for 10 or 12 persons.

Stew the apples in a jar, pass them through a hair sieve, and stir the pulp into the hot syrup. When cold, add the lemon-juice, and freeze. A few drops of carmine or cochineal improve the colour.

CHERRY WATER ICE.

With 1½ lb. of good cooking cherries, take 1½ pints of syrup (p. 118), 1 tablespoonful of lemon-juice, 1 tablespoonful of Kirsch (if liked), and carmine. Sufficient for 8 or 9 persons.

Stone the cherries, and from about a $\frac{1}{4}$ of the stones remove the kernels and pound them finely. Pour the syrup when boiling over the cherries and kernels, let it stand closely covered until cold, then add the Kirsch (if used), lemon-juice, and a few drops of carmine. Freeze as directed on p. 13.

GINGER WATER ICE.

Take 4 oz. of preserved ginger, a little of the syrup in which it is preserved, 1 pint of Syrup (p. 117), the stiffly-whisked white of 1 egg, the strained juice of 2 lemons and 1 orange, the rind of 1 orange, and 3 or 4 lumps of sugar. Sufficient for 6 or 7 persons.

Pound the ginger finely, adding gradually a little of its syrup, and press the whole through a fine sieve. Rub the sugar on the orange-rind, add the sugar to the ginger, together with the syrup, lemon and orange juices, and 3 tablespoonfuls of cold water. Boil up, strain, and, when cold, freeze (*see* p. 13), adding the white of egg when the mixture is about half frozen.

GRAPE WATER ICE.

To 1 lb. of sweetwater grapes, allow the thin rind of 2 lemons, the juice of 4 lemons, $1\frac{1}{2}$ pints of Syrup (p. 117), and 1 tablespoonful of orange-flower water.

Crush the grapes on a hair sieve, and press the pulp through with a wooden spoon, add the syrup boiling, lemon-rind and juice, let it remain until cold, then strain, add the orange-flower water, and freeze.

LEMON WATER ICE.

With $1\frac{1}{2}$ pints of Syrup (p. 117), take 6 lemons and 2 oranges. Sufficient for 7 or 8 persons.

Remove the peel from the lemons and 1 orange as thinly as possible, and place it in a basin. Make the syrup as directed, pour it boiling hot over the rinds, cover, and let it remain thus until cool, then add the juice of the lemons and oranges. Strain or tammy, and freeze.

MELON WATER ICE.

Procure 1 medium-sized ripe melon, 4 oz. of sugar, the juice of 2 oranges, the juice of 2 lemons, and 1 quart of water. Sufficient for about 8 persons.

Peel and slice the melon, simmer for 10 minutes with the water and sugar, and rub through a fine hair sieve. When cool, add the strained orange and lemon-juice, and, if necessary, a little more sugar. Freeze as directed on p. 13.

PEACH SHERBET.

Have ready 6 peaches, the juice of 4 lemons, sugar to taste, and 3 quarts of water. Sufficient for 3 quarts.

Skin and stone the fruit, remove the kernels from the stones, and chop them finely. Cut the fruit into small pieces, add the water, kernels, lemon-juice and sugar to taste. Let it remain on ice for 5 or 6 hours, and strain before using.

PINEAPPLE WATER ICE.

Take 1 preserved pineapple, 1 pint of Syrup (see below), and the juice of 1 lemon. Sufficient for 5 or 6 persons.

Make the syrup as directed. Pound the pineapple or chop it finely, and pass it through a hair sieve. Mix with it the syrup, add the lemon-juice, let the mixture become sufficiently cold, and freeze.

RASPBERRY OR STRAWBERRY WATER ICE.

To 1½ lb. of ripe strawberries or raspberries, allow 1½ pints of Syrup No. 1 (see below) and the juice of 2 lemons.

Prepare the syrup as directed. Rub the fruit through a fine sieve, add the lemon-juice, and if necessary deepen the colour with a few drops of carmine. Freeze as directed on p. 13.

RED-CURRANT WATER ICE.

With 1 lb. of red-currants, take ½ a lb. of raspberries, 1 quart of Syrup No. 1 (see below) and the juice of 1 lemon. Sufficient for 7 or 8 persons.

Pick the fruit and rub it through a hair sieve. Prepare the syrup according to the recipe, pour it over the fruit pulp, add the strained lemon-juice, and, when cold, freeze.

SYRUP FOR WATER ICES, No. 1.

Put 2 lb. of loaf sugar and 1 pint of water into a copper sugar-boiler or stewpan; when dissolved place over a clear fire, and boil until a syrup is formed, taking care to remove the scum as it rises. If a saccharometer is available for testing the heat of the syrup, it should be boiled until it registers 220° F. Sufficient for a pint of syrup.

SYRUP FOR WATER ICES, No. 2.

Procure 3 lb. of loaf sugar, 1 good pinch of cream of tartar, 1 quart of water, and the white and shell of 1 egg. Sufficient for 1 quart of syrup.

Place the sugar, cream of tartar, water, the shell and well-whisked white of egg in a copper sugar boiler or stewpan, boil until reduced to a syrup, then strain; when cool, use as required.

TANGERINE WATER ICE.

Take 6 tangerines, 2 oranges, 2 lemons, 2 oz. of loaf sugar, and 1 pint of Syrup (p. 117). Sufficient for 6 or 7 persons.

Rub the sugar on the rind of the tangerines to extract some of the flavour. Place the sugar in a saucepan, add the thin rind of 1 orange and 1 lemon, ¼ of a pint of cold water, and boil the mixture for 10 minutes. Skim if necessary, add the juice of the oranges and lemons, and the syrup, boil up, then strain, and, when cold, freeze.

WATER ICE MADE FROM JAM.

Have ready ½ a lb. of jam, 2 oz. of icing sugar, 1 pint of water, the juice of 1 lemon, and liquid colouring. Sufficient for 1½ pints.

Put all these ingredients together in a stewpan, bring to the boil, skim well, and simmer gently for 10 minutes. Now tammy or rub through a very fine hair sieve, add a few drops of colouring matter to brighten the colour, and, when cold, freeze.

SORBETS, MOUSSES AND ICED PUDDINGS

CHAMPAGNE GRANITE.

Prepare 1 quart of Lemon Water Ice (p. 116), and take ½ a bottle of champagne or saumure, ½ a lb. of fresh fruit, such as strawberries, apricots, peaches, all cut into small dice, and ½ a pint of crushed ice. Sufficient for 10 to 12 persons.

Prepare and freeze the lemon water ice, and stir in the champagne, prepared fruit and crushed ice. Serve in glasses or cups.

COFFEE ICED.

Make 1 quart of strong, clear, hot coffee, and take ½ a pint of milk, ½ a pint of cream, 6 oz. of castor sugar, and 1 inch of vanilla pod. Sufficient for 7 or 8 persons.

Place the milk, sugar and vanilla in a stewpan, bring nearly to boiling-point, then add the coffee, and let the mixture cool. Now strain, stir in the cream, freeze until it has the consistency of thick cream, and serve in this condition. Castor sugar should be handed with the coffee.

COFFEE PARFAIT.

Take 1 tablespoonful of coffee extract, 3 or 4 yolks of eggs, 1½ oz. of castor sugar, 1½ gills of Syrup (p. 117), and ¾ of a pint of cream. Sufficient for 7 or 8 persons.

Put the coffee extract, yolks of eggs, sugar and syrup into a stewpan, place it in a tin containing boiling water, and whisk the contents until they thicken. The mixture should be strongly flavoured with coffee, therefore add more essence if necessary, and let the mixture cool. Whip the cream stiffly, stir in lightly, pour the mixture into an ice mould, cover closely (see p. 13), and pack in ice for 2 or 3 hours.

Note.—With slight variations a large number of parfaits may be based on the above recipe. For Parfait au Thé, ½ a gill of very strong tea is substituted for the coffee extract : Parfait au Chocolat may be flavoured with 3 or 4 oz. of grated chocolate dissolved in a little milk ; Parfait aux Abricots or Parfait aux Pêches have pulped fruit added as a flavouring ingredient. Maraschino and Kirsch also enter largely into the composition of this particular class of sweet, the parfait, as a matter of course, taking its name from the liqueur.

CREAM SORBET.

With ½ a pint of cream, take ½ a lb. of loaf sugar, 1 oz. of vanilla sugar, the whites of 3 eggs, the juice of 2 lemons, and 1½ pints of water. Sufficient for 7 or 8 persons.

Add the loaf sugar to 1½ pints of boiling water, reduce a little by boiling rapidly, skimming frequently meanwhile, and add the lemon-juice. Strain, and thoroughly cool, then stir in the vanilla sugar, stiffly-whipped cream, and well-whisked whites of eggs. Freeze to the required consistency, and serve.

FROZEN PUDDING. (*See* Iced Queen's Pudding, p. 120, and Nesselrode Pudding, p. 122.)

GOOSEBERRY SORBET WITH MARASCHINO.

To 1 pint of green gooseberries, allow 6 oz. of loaf sugar, ½ a pint of water, the juice of 2 lemons, ½ a gill of Maraschino (optional), glacé cherries, and spinach colouring. Sufficient for 6 or 7 persons.

Pick the gooseberries, put them into a stewpan with the water and sugar, cook until tender, and rub through a hair sieve. Add the lemon-juice and spinach colouring until the desired shade of green is obtained. When cold, stir in the Maraschino (if used), freeze partially, and serve in small glasses tastefully garnished with strips of glacé cherries.

GRAPE SORBET.

Have ready 1 pint of half-frozen Lemon Water Ice (p. 116), 2 dozen large ripe green grapes, ½ a wineglassful of sherry or Marsala, and 1 wineglassful of elder-flower water. Sufficient for 6 or 7 persons.

Pass the grapes through a hair sieve, add them to the lemon-water ice when half frozen, and mix in the wine and elder-flower water. Continue the freezing a few minutes longer, until the whole is in a half-frozen condition. Serve in sorbet cups or glasses.

ICED PUDDING. (*See* Iced Queen's Pudding, p. 120, and Nesselrode Pudding, p. 122.)

ICED QUEEN'S PUDDING.

Prepare 1½ pints of Custard No. 1 (p. 109), and take 1 pint of cream, 2 oz. of crystallized apricots shredded or cut into dice, and 2 oz. of crystallized glacé cherries shredded or cut into dice, almonds. Sufficient for 8 persons.

Prepare the custard as directed ; when half frozen add the cream stiffly whipped and the prepared fruit, and press into a fancy ice mould. Cover, seal the edges with lard, wrap in paper, and pack in ice and salt for about 2 hours. Blanch, coarsely chop and bake the almonds brown, let them become perfectly cold, and sprinkle them lightly on the pudding just before serving.

LEMON GRANITE.

With 1 quart of half-frozen Lemon Water Ice (p. 116), take ½ a pint of finely-crushed ice and 1 small glass of Maraschino.

Add the crushed ice and Maraschino to the half-frozen lemon water ice, mix thoroughly, and serve in small cups or glasses.

LEMON SORBET.

Procure 8 lemons, 2 oranges, 8 oz. of loaf sugar, 2 oz. of castor sugar, 2 whites of eggs, and 3 pints of water. Sufficient for 8 persons.

Place the loaf sugar in a stewpan with the 3 pints of water; let it dissolve, then boil and reduce a little, and skim well during the process. Add the finely-grated rind of 2 lemons, the juice of the lemons and oranges, bring to the boil, strain, and let the preparation cool. Partially freeze, then add the well-whisked whites of eggs, and sugar, and continue the freezing (*see* instructions, p. 13) until the desired consistency is obtained.

Note.—For orange sorbet use 8 oranges and 2 lemons instead of 8 lemons and 2 oranges.

MARASCHINO MOUSSE.

Take 1 small glass each of Maraschino and Kirschwasser, ½ a pint of cream, ¼ of a pint of water, 4 oz. of loaf sugar, and 3 yolks of eggs. Sufficient for 6 or 7 persons.

Boil the 4 oz. of sugar and ¼ of a pint of water to a syrup, skimming meanwhile. Stir in the beaten yolks of eggs, add the Maraschino and Kirschwasser, and whisk the contents of the basin over a saucepan of boiling water until they thicken. Let the mixture cool, stirring frequently, and when ready to use add the stiffly-whipped cream. Line a plain mould with white paper, pour in the preparation, and cover closely, first with paper, and then with the lid. Pack in ice and salt for at least 2 hours.

MILK PUNCH.

To 1 quart of milk, allow 4 oz. of loaf sugar, 1 gill of cream, and 2 tablespoonfuls of brandy or rum. Sufficient for 7 or 8 persons.

Boil the milk, dissolve the sugar in it, then strain, and, when cool, partially freeze. Add the brandy or rum, and the cream whipped, mix well, and freeze a little longer. Serve in a half-frozen condition in small china sorbet-cups, and, if liked, grate on a little nutmeg or cinnamon before serving.

NEAPOLITAN ICE.

Have ready ¼ of a pint of strawberry or raspberry pulp, ½ an oz. of grated chocolate, 3 yolks of eggs, 1½ pints of milk, ½ a pint of cream, 3 oz. of castor sugar, ½ a teaspoonful of vanilla essence, and carmine. Sufficient for 7 or 8 persons.

Cream the yolks of eggs and 3 oz. of castor sugar well together. Boil the milk and pour it on to the yolks of eggs and sugar, stirring vigorously meanwhile. Replace in the stewpan, and stir by the side of the fire until the mixture thickens, then strain. Dissolve the chocolate in 1 table-spoonful of water, mix with it a third of the custard, and let it cool. Mix the fruit pulp with half the remaining custard, and if necessary add a few drops of carmine. To the other third of the custard add the vanilla essence. Whip the cream slightly, divide it into three equal portions, and add one to each preparation. Freeze separately, then pack in layers in a Neapolitan ice-box, or, failing this, a mould best suited to the purpose. Cover closely, and pack in salt and ice for about 2 hours. Serve cut across in slices.

NESSELRODE PUDDING.

Procure 3 dozen chestnuts, ½ a pint of milk, 1 pint of cream, 8 oz. of loaf sugar, 2 oz. of glacé cherries cut into dice, 4 or 5 yolks of eggs, and vanilla essence. Sufficient for 9 or 10 persons.

Shell, parboil, and skin the chestnuts, simmer them in 1 gill of milk until tender, and rub them through a fine sieve. Bring the remaining gill of milk nearly to boiling-point, add the yolks of eggs, cook by the side of the fire until they thicken, then stir them into the chestnut purée. Let this mixture become cold, add half the cream, freeze until nearly set, then stir in the cherries, and the remainder of the cream stiffly-whipped. Freeze until set, stirring frequently, then press into a fancy ice mould, cover, seal the edges with lard, wrap in paper, and bury in ice and salt until required.

PARFAITS. (*See* **Coffee Parfait**, p. 119.)

PEACH MELBA.

With 4 or 5 firm, ripe peaches, take ½ a gill of raspberry syrup, ½ a pint of Vanilla ice cream (p. 114), 4 oz. of sugar, and vanilla flavouring. Sufficient for 4 or 5 persons.

Halve and peel the peaches, and poach them in a syrup flavoured with vanilla until tender but not broken. Lift out the peaches, drain them on a sieve, and let them get thoroughly cold. Serve them piled around a mound of vanilla ice cream in a silver dish. Set this in another dish containing shaved ice. Pour over a rich raspberry syrup, which must be previously iced. Serve at once.

PINEAPPLE MOUSSE.

To 10 oz. of preserved pineapple, allow 2 oz. of castor sugar, ¾ of an oz. of gelatine, ½ a gill of pineapple syrup, 1½ gills of cream, ¼ of a gill of Maraschino (if liked), 1½ gills of Lemon or Wine jelly (pp. 55 and 60), and glacé cherries. Sufficient for 6 or 7 persons.

Mask the jelly-mould with a thin layer of jelly, and decorate with the cherries. Pound and chop the pineapple finely, and rub it through a hair sieve. Dissolve the sugar and gelatine in the pineapple syrup, and let the mixture cool. Melt the remainder of the jelly ; let it cool, and whisk it over the ice to a stiff froth. Add this and the stiffly-whipped cream to the pineapple purée, stir in the gelatine when cool, add the Maraschino (if used), and pour into the prepared mould. Let it remain on ice for 2 hours.

QUEEN'S PUDDING, ICED. (*See* Iced Queen's Pudding, p. 120.)

RASPBERRY SOUFFLÉ, ICED. (*See* Strawberry and Raspberry Soufflé, Iced, p. 124.)

ROMAN PUNCH.

Take 1 lb. of loaf sugar, 1 quart of water, 6 lemons, 2 oranges, 3 whites of eggs, and ¼ of a pint of rum or cherry-water. Sufficient for 7 or 8 persons.

Place the water and sugar in a copper sugar boiler or stewpan, and boil to a syrup. Add the thinly-cut rind of 3 lemons and 1 orange, the orange and lemon-juice, and bring to the boil. When cold, strain, partially freeze, then add the rum or cherrywater, the stiffly-whisked whites of eggs, and freeze for a few minutes longer. Serve in a half-frozen condition in sorbet cups or glasses.

STRAWBERRY OR RASPBERRY SOUFFLÉ, ICED.

Have ready 1 gill of strawberry or raspberry pulp, ½ a pint of cream, 6 oz. of castor sugar, ½ an oz. of leaf gelatine, 2 lemons, 2 yolks of eggs, 2 whites of eggs, ¼ of a gill of Lemon or Wine jelly (pp. 55 and 60), and ¼ of a gill of red-currant jelly. Sufficient for 6 or 7 persons.

Add the sugar, the juice and finely-grated rinds of the lemons to the yolks of eggs, and whisk over a saucepan of boiling water until the mixture thickens. Add the gelatine previously dissolved in 1 tablespoonful of water, and the fruit pulp, let the mixture cool, then stir in the well-whisked whites of eggs and the stiffly-whipped cream. Have ready a silver-plated soufflé-dish with a band of strong white paper raised about 2 inches above the rim, pour in the mixture, and let it stand on ice for about 2 hours. Melt the lemon or wine and red-currant jellies, let them cool, and as soon as the surface of the soufflé is firm, pour them over. To serve : remove the band of paper, and send to table in the soufflé-dish.

INDEX

LEA & PERRINS' SAUCE

is a concentrated

essence of spices. It is the

ideal flavouring for all

SOUPS, GRAVIES & MEAT DISHES

"She's been picked for *Batchelor's* where the best *Peas* go!"

B.P. 13/814

a joint success

STUFFO

Ready-to-use stuffing in 2 Packings—
SAGE & ONION, PARSLEY & THYME

PREPARED HERBS

in handy packets—MIXED HERBS,
SAGE, MINT, PARSLEY, THYME, etc.

Ask for them at leading Greengrocers,
Grocers, etc. and look for the Trade Mark.
Established 1868

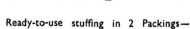

PANNETT & NEDEN STEWARTS RD., LONDON. S.W.8,
HERB FARM, CARSHALTON, SURREY.

Lightning Source UK Ltd.
Milton Keynes UK
UKOW051410280112

186209UK00001B/6/A